POLIO

A PERSONAL SPIRITUAL JOURNEY

How a Physical Difference Impacts One's Life
Trajectory in Challenging and Decisive Ways

by Robert W. Janek

DORRANCE PUBLISHING CO
EST. 1920
PITTSBURGH, PENNSYLVANIA 15238

The contents of this work, including, but not limited to, the accuracy of events, people, and places depicted; opinions expressed; permission to use previously published materials included; and any advice given or actions advocated are solely the responsibility of the author, who assumes all liability for said work and indemnifies the publisher against any claims stemming from publication of the work.

All Rights Reserved
Copyright © 2023 by Robert W. Janek

No part of this book may be reproduced or transmitted, downloaded, distributed, reverse engineered, or stored in or introduced into any information storage and retrieval system, in any form or by any means, including photocopying and recording, whether electronic or mechanical, now known or hereinafter invented without permission in writing from the publisher.

Dorrance Publishing Co
585 Alpha Drive
Pittsburgh, PA 15238
Visit our website at *www.dorrancebookstore.com*

ISBN: 979-8-8872-9447-6
eISBN: 979-8-8872-9947-1

POLIO
A PERSONAL SPIRITUAL JOURNEY

How a Physical Difference Impacts One's Life
Trajectory in Challenging and Decisive Ways

Dedicated to my wife, Jena
through whose tireless and patient efforts
this book was made possible.

CONTENTS

Preface xi
Definitions Used and Questioned 1
Introduction 5
The Beginning 11
The Journey 19
Spiritual Reflections 81
Appendix (Polio Medical Records) 111
Biographical Information 119

"But men see differently. I can at best report only from my own wilderness." [1]

— Loren Eiseley

PREFACE

I had bulbar polio in the summer of 1952 when I was barely eleven years old.

As I share in these pages my personal life story with polio and how it has affected my life journey, I have three primary audiences in mind. The first is those caregivers (clergy, therapists, social workers, counselors, family members) who work on an everyday basis with people who live with physical handicaps or who have "visible physical anomalies" (VPAs, that is, noticeable physical differences) that set them apart from "normals." Hopefully, in some small way, what I have to say here will help caregivers better understand and appreciate the life journey challenges of those with VPAs.

The second audience is those people who themselves possess visible physical anomalies or physical disabilities who find that their personal experiences—such as inner struggles encountering the world, their beliefs, and their personal shaken sense of purpose and place in the world—do not seem to fit much of the "inspirational" religious material they read. They tend to feel as if they are failures and inadequate to the task of being human with a "differentness" because they don't measure up to the Christian devotional biographies of others who seem to have "overcome" their problems through extraordinary faith or strong belief. Hopefully, what I have to say will reassure them that it is okay to be human, it's okay to admit that daily they have to face challenges that, at times, can feel overwhelming; it's okay to feel discouraged and lonely at times; it's okay to experience what one female veteran battling rheumatoid arthritis once shared with me: "Chaplain, at times I feel combat fatigue!"

Finally, a third audience could be identified as "posterity" or history...or tragically, the newcomers in 2022 who are experiencing the re-emergence of this life-interrupting disease, polio. We polio survivors of the '30s, '40s, and '50s era are aging and dying. Like old war veterans of a long ago largely forgotten war, we are disappearing from the landscape of history. Are we now frighteningly seeing a resurgence of that old "enemy"?

DEFINITIONS USED AND QUESTIONED

In my story, I use the term "anomaly" instead of handicap or disability because the latter terms usually denote an inability to be able to do certain things physically; and not all physical anomalies restrict one's physical ability. Further, I use the term "visible" physical anomaly to denote physical differences, such as facial paralysis, that can be immediately seen and reacted to by others. As Beatrice Wright said:

> ... With some impairments, as in facial disfigurement, the handicapping factors reside entirely in negative social and personal attitudes insofar as the disfigurement itself does not involve a functional loss.[2]

At times, I catch myself wanting to characterize the facial paralysis as a "visible physical *stigma*," using Erving Goffman's definition or concept of "stigma":

> ...an individual who might have been received easily in ordinary social intercourse possesses a trait that can obtrude itself upon attention and turn those of us whom he meets away from him, breaking the claim that his other attributes have on us.[3]

1

Among other things, "handicap" or "disability" can occur from within and/or from without an individual. It can be from *within* when and if the person feels somehow handicapped or limited or in some way unusually disabled or if she/he feels more limited than that person really is or need be. It is a form of self-limitation.

"Handicaps" can occur from *without* if others place the person in a handicapped mold or role, that is, if they treat him or her as being, in some way, disabled or limited or handicapped. This attitude, at best, has a negative effect; at worst, a devastating, stunting effect upon the life potential of the person placed in that mold. The person is forced by others to live a more limited lifestyle than the person is actually capable of living. It can become a very frustrating and dehumanizing category or "pigeon-hole" to be placed in; one which can drain away the initiative and energy to live at one's potential...to even *strive* toward one's potential. For example, in many ways, the person with a visible physical anomaly may not be allowed to reach...or even seek...that person's greatest potential. "Normals," or people who do not have VPAs, notice and are repulsed by the physical anomaly, and then reject that person just because she/he does not look "normal," without giving that person the opportunity to prove his/her worth or ability. In this sense, the VPA becomes handicapped or disabled from without, by being labeled "handicapped" by others.

At times, I think that I perceive a rather insidious attitude by some "normals": the unstated and unwritten demand that the "handicapped" or the VPA person should be acutely aware of his or her "place" in the pecking order, and stay in it! Again, Beatrice Wright:

> Underprivileged status may be insisted upon by those who want minority-group members not only to know their place but also to <u>keep</u> their place – that is, to feel and act less fortunate than others.[4]

I find that those who have VPAs often fall into a kind of social limbo: they are not considered "physically handicapped," which they are usually not, and yet they are not considered "normal," either. This psycho-social "limbo-location" was brought home to me one day when the secretary of the office where I worked suggested that I list myself as "Handicapped" so that our office could show that we have *two* handicapped persons working in it! It would give us "points" in the head office! I must admit that her sincerely meant suggestion threw me off balance. I didn't quite know how to handle it.

On another occasion, I was asked by members of a committee within the hospital that annually chose a "Handicapped Employee of the Year" if I would accept their nomination for such an honor. I felt uncomfortable. I turned it down, because I did not believe that facial paralysis was a physical handicap or limited my ability to do my job as a hospital chaplain. In a sort of an answer that I typed up, I asked:

> The agonizing question is: How do we define "handicap" or "disability" or "physically challenged" or whatever...?
>
> - Does this include those of us who may look "different"?
> - What about burn victims who are physically disfigured, but otherwise function normally?
> - What about over-weight people? ...Those of us who are balding?
>
> Do you—the committee—see me as a handicapped person? In WHAT WAY do you believe that I am handicapped? Is facial paralysis due to childhood polio to be considered a handicap/disability/physical challenge? In what way? How does this affect your attitude toward me?
>
> - Are those employees who are truly physically

handicapped going to feel angry that a non-handicapped person received the award?

We, as a society, are caught up in a kind of paradox toward the handicapped/"different." On the one hand we try to encourage people to respect and to see such individuals as worthy human beings with abilities and talents just like "normals." On the other hand, medical science strives to conquer these very same handicaps/differences, in essence sending the message that these "differences" are NOT OKAY.

In this story, I cannot speak for other "polio survivors." As Loren Eiseley said, "I can at best report only from my own wilderness."[5]

INTRODUCTION

Years ago, as I was paying the cashier in a Kansas City, Missouri, restaurant, she asked, "Where are you traveling from?" The question intrigued me all the way back to Leavenworth that day: "Yes, where am I traveling *from*? Well, young lady, why don't we sit down over a cup of coffee and I'll tell you where I'm traveling *from!*"

Where does one begin to tell a personal story like this? I was born in Fort Worth, Texas, in July 1941, was adopted in infancy by a southwest Texas dry-land farmer and his school-teacher wife, and grew up amid the cotton and milo fields of "Lipan Flats" near San Angelo in Tom Green County. Except for a few distant hills along the horizon, the land is flat: there are no mountains or forests to block a person's view of the brilliant sunrises and the burnt orange sunsets. Like snowflakes, no two are alike. On moonless nights, the inky-black sky, bisected by the millions of stars of the "Milky Way," curved over this farm country like an upside-down bowl. Rain, or the lack thereof, started, and often ended, conversations between farmers: upon it depended this year's crop.

The first ten years of my life were fairly normal dry-land farm-kid growing-up years. "The War" had ended; a cousin, who had fought in

Europe with the 3rd Armored Division, came to live with us for several months, and my brother and I were given wooden guns that our cousin had carved out of wood. My education in Wall, Texas, commenced in a classroom next to the school's lunchroom, both of which were behind the stage in the school's auditorium. My mother, Eda Lisso Janek, was my first teacher.... She would go on to teach first grade there at Wall School for thirty years until her retirement in 1976. Both my mother and my father were very active in school affairs and were instrumental in eventually making Wall a twelve-year high school. For the most part, all of the students in that school were farm-raised kids; we thus had much in common. I grew up in an "extended-family" environment, with maternal grandparents, uncles, aunts, and cousins living in not-too-distant communities, families that we visited often.

Then came 1952, when my life took a drastic turn. Early that year, at age ten, I was stricken with a case of appendicitis and underwent an appendectomy at the old Clinic Hospital on West Beauregard, a procedure from which, I found out years later, I almost died. Then, later that year, I spent nearly four weeks in the same hospital with bulbar polio. The polio, and the consequent paralysis on the left side of my face, would have a profound impact upon the direction of my life, on how I would see and understand life. While, fortunately, I never had to deal with an iron lung or leg braces, I would wrestle with intense inner psycho-spiritual pain and turmoil relating to selfhood, the curious stares and cruel remarks of others, and a certain sadness at being "different." Through it all (and perhaps because of it?), I went on to finish high school in 1959, graduated from Texas Tech College (now, University) with a Bachelor of Arts degree in government and history in 1964, and was commissioned into the Army through ROTC. I spent four years in the Army, including one year, 1966–1967, in Viet Nam as an advisor. I left the Army as a captain in armor. I then went to work as a civilian intelligence analyst with the Defense Intelligence Agency in Washington, DC, and remained there for five years. While there, I did graduate work in international relations at American University. During all of those years, I quietly struggled with a myriad of philosophical and theological questions about the meaning of life in the face of the problem of suffering and "differentness," a struggle that forced its way to the surface of my life in 1973, leading me to decide to enter seminary. I attended the Iliff School of Theology in Denver (a United Methodist seminary), completing a Master of Divinity Degree in specialized ministry and a Master of Arts in Religion Degree in the philosophy of religion and Christian theology. In addition to the seminary education, I completed four units (a hospital chaplaincy internship) of Clinical Pastoral Education at M. D. Anderson Hospital and Tumor Institute in Houston, and four more units (a residency) at Wesley Medical Center in Wichita, Kansas. While in seminary, I would meet and marry another seminary student, Jena Bircher, and a few years later, would adopt our son, Daryl, who, with his wife Mary, currently lives in the midst of the Green Mountains of Vermont.

I went to seminary (and into the hospital chaplaincy) NOT because I somehow felt "called," but instead, because the pain of life pushed me to more openly pursue the search for answers to the deeply spiritual and existential questions I had been dealing with for years. This book reflects a part of that search…that journey.

Out of this continuing experience, I have made it one of my life's goals or values to reflect on suffering and then to adopt a personal value system, based on my own understanding of what it means to be a Christian, out of which I can, in some small way, make life a little more livable for others when they face their own difficult situations, and as a consequence, a little more livable for me. I have struggled (not always successfully) to use my "differentness" to become more sensitive to and understanding of others' pain, turning my personal woundedness into a kind of spiritual strength whereby I can attempt to be part of the solution rather than part of the problem of human existence.

Writing has been, and is, a therapy, a comfort, and a learning process for me as I reflect on my experiences, thoughts, and feelings. I would hope that my story in some small way can give courage and hope to those struggling with their own life-paralyzing dilemmas.

A Warning: This is *not* a book about a person who experienced some kind of profound spiritual or religious victory over polio and the consequent permanent facial paralysis, and who then went on with life as if nothing significant had happened! Permanent paralysis changes one permanently in many ways. When people with disabilities or physical anomalies deny any continuing struggle with their situation, I begin to wonder. I sense that they are either in a strong case of denial, or they are not being honest. Occasionally, apparently for religious reasons, such people will proclaim that they have "overcome" their handicap and no longer have to deal with it spiritually or emotionally. I must admit that this is difficult for me to believe. One is not the same person after such an experience as she/he was before the experience. I know that I was not the same person after the polio experience as I was before. Things just don't go back to "normal," if by that one means that things return to the way they were before the illness. Life is forever changed.

I always suspect that people are attracted to such inspirational, "all-is-cured" stories because they tend to absolve the reader of any responsibility. In these stories the handicapped or disabled or disfigured person has, supposedly with the help of God, become "normal" again, or has even become "saintly." Therefore, the reader need not learn of the pain of the human condition…need not learn about the continuing pain and struggles that the disabled and disfigured (even Christian) experiences, thinking:

- God has taken care of the problem, so I don't have to worry about attempting to understand the struggles that person, in actuality, continues to deal with on a daily basis.

- I don't have to sensitize myself to the social prejudices and biases that keep such people from living up to their full potential.

Such stories all too often elicit only feelings of sympathy for the "poor cripple" rather than a deeper understanding and appreciation and sensitivity for what people experience in life.

I would suggest that "overcoming" a permanent handicap, disability, or disfigurement does NOT mean that it "goes away" or disappears. To live life with such a "differentness" means learning to live life in a creative, contributive way. It means learning to accept oneself in spite of the "differentness"; that one is a valuable, lovable, worthwhile human being.

On the contrary, these are raw and honest reflections about life; life lived by one human being within the horizon of American society in the second half of the twentieth century and into the twenty-first century, a person who as a hospital chaplain has walked with many others struggling with disabilities and "differentness." This is a story in process…becoming…on the way. It is not a "happily-ever-after" kind of story all too often taught in Sunday school, because it is a story about real human life, the kind of life Christians *really* experience. It is not a story for those who are afraid to be honest with God; those who believe that a person (Christian) must present a certain pious image to God and to others. It is not a story for the squeamishly pious! It is a story in which I attempt to be "brutally honest," sharing with the reader how one particular person attempts to make sense out of a life lived with what I call a "visible physical anomaly" (facial paralysis due to polio). I firmly believe that we as Christians should face life as it is, not as we might wish it to be, for only then can we truly minister to one another in loving, redemptive, creative, contributive ways.

THE BEGINNING

As an eleven-year-old boy suddenly slammed by POLIO, I remember very little about the hospitalization itself. My memories, due to the fever/delirium, are surrealistic images. The night before, we went to a relative's house for what should have been a great supper (in the west Texas that I grew up in, "dinner" was the noon meal, "supper" was in the evening), and to share our family's experiences of a recent trip to Tennessee to visit other relatives. However, that night I felt horrible. I faintly remember initially being in a room somewhere in the old Clinic Hospital in San Angelo, Texas.

And then there are the broken images of the night—or was it daytime?—they did the tracheotomy. In my fevered mind, the surgery was taking place on the screened-in porch or "gallery" of my grandparents' ranch house in Concho County…and there was the doctor asking for a sponge. In what one could perhaps label as an "out-of-body" experience, I seemed to be hovering up against the ceiling above all of the action during the in-room surgery! (I vaguely remember someone once telling me that I was too weak to be anesthetized, so, apparently, they only gave me a "local" and then did the surgery in my hospital room!) There were the "hot pack" treatments: being stripped of all clothing, basted with baby oil, and wrapped in steamy, prickly Army blankets with rubber sheets placed over and under me to keep in the heat. I suspect that these "Sister Kenny" treatments warped my brain and made me morally handicapped! There were the Jell-O and ice cream that I was fed to test my ability to swallow. After all of those feedings in such a traumatic circumstance, it's a wonder that I still enjoy Jell-O and ice cream! And the feeding tubes and IVs which were excruciatingly painful. The IVs were boarded to my restless arm. There was a metal comb that I was allowed to keep afterwards because it could be disinfected and sterilized, while all else that I had in the room had to be destroyed, to include numerous toy train catalogs! There was the cousin, going off to Korea as an Air Force pilot, who, in his Air Force blue uniform, came to the basement window to say goodbye. Because he was not allowed to enter the basement, he came to my window and knelt down so that I could see him from my bed. What a gesture! The polio patients were kept in the basement of the hospital isolated from the rest of the world. Lepers! There was the red-and-silver Lionel Santa Fe Diesel my parents bought me for having survived the ordeal, and which I so foolishly sold many years later for a pittance! I still regret this! There were the monstrous recurring nightmares night after night after I returned home, coming at me like the bubbles in one of those lava lamps.

Years after my hospitalization, my mother, Eda Sarah Lisso Janek, wrote a letter describing her perspective of the experience:

A Mother's Memories of Polio — 1952

Robert, our 10 (sic) year old son, felt ill on Friday evening at a relative's home. We went home early, and I took him to our pediatrician early Saturday. He examined him, and sent us to X-Ray—to x-ray his face on the L. side—said it might be "Bell's

Palsy"— The technician told him to close his eyes— He said he couldn't close his left eye; so I said, "Just close it with your hand."

He was put to bed—high temp—on 2nd floor. A restless day, and a horrible night; he was delirious, and I had great difficulty keeping him in the bed. By morning I felt <u>sure</u> it had to be polio—

When the Dr. made his rounds, he told me they were going to do a spinal tap—

I sat in the lobby, talking to a lady who had 2 polio patients in the Hosp. basement. Panic was so near! His Dad came in during the wait, for results of the tap—

Finally, the Dr. called us into his office and told us it <u>was</u> polio, and, since the first symptoms were above his shoulders it would be bulbar, and, likely, another type, as well.

We were moved to the basement at once, where 15 other patients were. When he was settled in, I went home to get clothes; to remain in the room. The Dr. said nurses refused to serve with polio patients, and only <u>one</u> R.N., on the regular staff came to that basement—for day shifts. An aide came at nights— So, a member of a family was allowed to stay—and <u>needed</u> to.

The Dr. gave our older son a gamma-globulin injection the same Sunday. (He, the Dr. was one of the <u>few</u> medical professionals at that time who <u>believed</u> the injection was helpful).

Robert was delirious at that point—when I came back— (Having <u>had</u> to tell my elderly parents the diagnosis <u>was</u> polio—) I was back at his bed (elevated 1', at the foot) and having a difficult time keeping him on the bed—I stood beside him—holding him—and praying, and becoming more worried as the minutes passed.

The bulky suction machine was on the other side of the bed, and used by the nurse, at intervals, to suction the flow of mucus from his throat—By Tues—a nurse friend, had sent me some type of "No-doz" tablets, and the doctor said a neck-piece to adapt a lung to a child was due to be flown from Dallas by Wed.—It did not arrive, and by that evening, Robert was quieter, and I could sit by the bed. In my ignorance, I felt he was better—About 11:30 P.M. the Dr. came in, began vigorously suctioning his throat, and said they were going to do a tracheotomy as soon as a surgeon arrived—

They then wrapped his body tightly in a sheet, and performed the surgery in the room. I sat, with my husband—on the stairway just across the hall—in extreme anguish over the happening—

When the surgery was over, my husband and another man, whose wife (an R.N.) was in an iron lung in the adjoining room, found the mops, and cleaned up the blood on Robert's room floor—A nightmare, truly!

It seems disaster sometimes can be a blessing, in disguise—The fact that "neck-piece" (collar)—did not come—(and the tracheotomy did enable him to live—) kept him from the lung, and subsequent problems of getting him out of it—

I walked out in the back parking lot the next day, while the nurse stayed in Rob's room—

A beautiful Church adjoined the lot—and I tried the door, hoping it was open—but not so—some steps leading into the basement were open—I sat on those for a time—praying a turn had come—

The little aide had come in the room early—before dawn that day—and began to talk of her experiences in the ward—and the terrible consequences possible from the huge flow of mucus, of bulbar patients: I was horrified!—(to say the least). I realized now she should never have told me of the patients she'd seen die—But—she was very young—and it was all very traumatic, for her, as well.

The fever subsided over the weekend, and the "Sister Kenny"—hot blanket-treatments began—

Robert had been fed through a tube all this time—(and for over 3 weeks—) <u>Finally</u>, he was able to swallow—He talked, so often, of foods wished for—His speech was garbled—and difficult to understand—except for one word at a time.—<u>very</u> frustrating for him—

His body wasted away in a week's time—Unbelievably so!! He wasn't heavy before, but now just skin and bones. I could pick him up on the bed, like a baby—

As all polio victims, he abhorred the hot packs, and begged me to "read, read! read!" while wrapped up to his nose and eyes in those harsh, woolen army blankets.

A physical therapist began coming in after the second week, and worked with his left side. Moving his leg meant screams of pain, but he <u>was</u> able to walk out of the hospital after 33 days.

Then, a long period of nerve recovery, and continued therapy. We had to adjust to a child, now so easily disturbed and upset—Constant nightmares—instead of the calm, even tempered youngster he'd always been—In <u>time</u>, it gradually changed.

But the pain of seeing him have to adjust to "being different" in the perception of other people—children <u>and</u> adults—endures to this day. He has coped with it better than I have, it seems to me.

However, all of this trauma has made him a special person—perceptive, and understanding of the problems and trials of others.

Perhaps I should say—

"God moves in a mysterious way.
His Miracles to perform"—

P.S. It's been <u>difficult</u>, to recall these memories—<u>very</u> painful, even now, 35+ years later—[6]

In her own autobiographical sketches and notes, my mother wrote this account:

After we were home a couple of weeks, we were at Victor's (Urban) for a cook-out, and Robert said he had a headache, and didn't eat barbecue, so we came home early. Next morning, Saturday, he still felt badly, so I took him in to Dr. Finks. He was checked over, and finally sent to X-ray to look at his face—maybe "Bell's Palsy," etc. However, when told to close his eyes, he said, "The left one won't stay closed." Nurse covered it—and—-so—-he was eventually admitted to a bed and room on main floor. He WAS ill, so I stayed with him over night. He was VERY ill—high fever—-and Sunday AM when Bill came in the doctors said they feared it was polio, and were going to do a spinal tap to be sure.

It WAS—and we were told it would be bulbar polio (type) in which breathing is affected—in addition to other types. This, they could be positive of because first symptoms of paralysis appeared ABOVE his shoulders.

We were then moved to a large room in the basement of Clinic Hospital. All rooms were filled with polio patients (12 or 13). A former nurse (A PATIENT) was there, was in a room next to us, in an iron lung. Only ONE nurse (RN?) was on that floor (from 7 – 3)—the rest, just AIDES!! Nurses REFUSED to work in polio wards that summer! The iron lung patient had 2 very elderly retired nurses, who took turns taking care of her.

Family members stayed with the others; however. All were not critically ill, depending on the type of polio they had.

Robert's temperature was high—delirious at times, and a suction machine was placed in the room to suction mucus from his throat, at intervals—a GREAT amount of this formed; removed by cupfuls—-a clear, clinging type of mucus that couldn't be brought up nor spit out. It seemed to surge and flow, at times. Blocks were placed under his bed at the foot to raise it at least a foot—-to keep his lungs clearing if possible. He thrashed about constantly—-and had to be lifted and moved—-to stay on the bed. He wasn't heavy, and in a couple of days, his body was just skin and bones—-due to the disease.

On Wednesday AM they decided he needed to go into an iron lung but one for a child wasn't available in San Angelo: a foam neckpiece was needed., to be able to use a large lung for a child. Dallas was called, and one was to be flown in that afternoon. It failed to come.

I sat by him that evening late, and he became much quieter than he'd ever been. In my ignorance of polio, I thought he was better. But near 12:00 (MIDNIGHT) Dr. Finks came in, and said, "This is BAD! He's slipping away!!" He sent the aid to call Dr. Engelking—and he began to use the suction machine desperately to clear his lungs. Dr. Engelking came in minutes, and they wrapped Robert in a sheet, like a mummy and Dr. Engelking did a tracheotomy as quickly as possible right there in the room.

Bill and Mr. Snow (the iron-lung-patient's husband) were sitting on the basement steps. THEY got mops and buckets and cleaned up the room after the surgery. It was truly a night mare!"

Robert's throat was paralyzed after Sunday, so now a feeding tube was placed in his nose, and remained for 3 weeks until he was, AT LAST, able to swallow. The trachea tube made suctioning easier, and by the second week, hot packs (Sister Kenny method) were begun. A steam tub was placed in the room, and woolen army blankets placed in it. Then Robert was wrapped in them for 30 minute intervals several times a day. Only his nose and eyes were out. I read NON-STOP to him during these times.

The last week or so, a physical therapist came in daily to work with him. His left side was paralyzed—arms, legs didn't bend or move—but with hot packs and massage it finally worked out.

Thirty days after it began, he came home—left side of his face paralyzed, and a very rough ugly scar from the trachea opening, but with time, it went away. He went in for therapy for several months—six months, I believe, to SHELLY SMITH, who now heads the "Rehab" Centers at Abilene and San Angelo.

In mid-October, Robert entered school, but nerve damage was long in healing. He was easily upset—as NEVER before; had nightmares, and extra exertion took its toll for quite a period of time. POLIO—a curse to thousands!![7]

THE JOURNEY

For those permanently paralyzed by polio, the hospital phase is really just the beginning of a long, bumpy, and challenging journey. With the polio experience, and the resulting facial paralysis, my world began to change. As I now reflect upon that experience and its aftermath, I can see that I began to gradually view the world, and life, differently: differently from my peer group, and differently from the way I had previously viewed it. I began to have to create a different set of values and priorities by which to live my life. Hugh Gallagher observed:

> I have never met any person for whom the paralysis was not a vital – if not the most vital – shaping event of his life. These polios are as scarred by their experience as concentration camp survivors are scarred by theirs.[8]

As much as I wanted to be like my peers in the small rural school in southwest Texas (Wall), which I attended from first through the twelfth grades, I began to realize that, in one significant respect at least, I was "different" because of the facial paralysis. This "differentness" was quickly, and painfully, brought to my attention in various ways shortly after I was discharged from the hospital, and would continue throughout my life in what I would describe as "encounters of the uncomfortable kind."

Several months after my hospitalization, my dad and I went to a special clinic for "crippled children," which was held in San Angelo. It was set up to help, but I hated being there! It made me "one of them": somehow a freak of the human race…somehow not totally whole or complete or normal. As I looked around at all the other "freaks," I felt miserable, ashamed, exposed, vulnerable, inferior, humiliated. I wanted to crawl into a hole, not to be seen there by my friends. And yet, I was helpless to change things: I WAS "one of them"!

Many years later (July 1994) when I shared this incident with a group of substance abuse patients in a Veterans Administration (VA) medical center, one of the patients responded by saying that I should not have felt this shame and humiliation, but that, instead, in the face of the fact that many children were dying of polio in 1952, I should have felt like a miracle. Of course, very few eleven-year-old children understand the concept of miracles! Further, if I use his line of reasoning, then logically I could say that it would have been a "miracle" if I had not contracted polio in the first place! Also, why didn't God work a "miracle" on those children who DID die and those who were more severely affected by polio than I was? To respond to these kinds of questions by saying that we cannot understand the ways of God is, to me, an intellectual "cop-out." However, I realize that he was attempting to see the positive or the "bright" side of my childhood experience; but his approach was not really good pastoral care. Instead of affirming me in my feelings, he was unconsciously setting me up to feel guilty that I had such feelings (of shame and humiliation) in the first place!

In the months following my hospitalization, in one of the experimental attempts to regain some muscle control in my face, it was suggested that I chew a lot of gum on the left paralyzed side! Thus, for months I chewed bubblegum—I think it was Fleers—and was the only student in my class allowed to do so during class! With all of that sugar, it's a wonder that I have any teeth left! Here was another indication that I was "different" from the normal kids.

Along with chewing the bubblegum, I went to a physical therapist who attempted to restore some of my muscle control with a kind of electrode device that he held up to the left side of my face…; it tingled, but was not successful.

During the next several years after contracting polio, my "differentness" was forcefully brought to my attention when visiting relatives, cousins who lived on a farm not far from ours. Normally, in the past when we were there visiting, neighbor children would walk across the cotton and milo fields to play with us. However, now that I was "tainted" with polio, their parents would not allow them to be around me: the leper! People were horribly frightened of polio, and of anyone who had had it.

On another occasion, a few years later as I became more romantically inclined, I was attending a high school basketball game at a neighboring school and sitting next to my girlfriend. I was having a great time, feeling on top of the world…euphoric…feeling a part of the world, a part of humanity. I was not conscious of how public my facial paralysis was! I happened to glance over my shoulder and noticed a student from the opposing school imitating my facial paralysis to the delight of other students who laughed along with him. I felt as if I had been pierced by a white-hot spear; and there was not a thing in the world that I could do about it. I felt helpless…angry…humiliated…worthless…ashamed. I wanted to run and hide somewhere…to run away from life! I no longer wanted to be a part of life, but instead, apart *from* life! How could this beautiful girl stand to be sitting with me in public?!

There was another time during those growing-up years, at another sports event, when an acquaintance was showing me the picture of a school friend of hers. I mentioned that the friend's smile seemed to reach from ear to ear, intending it as a compliment. However, she interpreted it otherwise, and lashed out in savage, cutting anger: "At least *she* has a smile!" Devastation! A crushing blow! How does one respond? Turn away, wounded.

Personal life stories, and "encounters of the uncomfortable kind," do not come to an end at the end of childhood.

Several years, and many experiences and encounters later, when I was involved in Clinical Pastoral Education at M. D. Anderson Hospital (1975–1976), I had a couple more such encounters. One day I was in a room visiting a patient when a doctor walked in and noticed my facial paralysis.

"Stroke?" he innocently asked.

His remark, which caught me off balance and unprepared psychologically, made me defensively furious: "I would think that you, a doctor, would know about polio!"

I normally don't go around every minute of the day thinking of or conscious of my facial paralysis; thus, his observation was another reminder that I was indeed "different"; and it was a threat to my ego, to my self-esteem, to my sense of self-worth! His observation forced me to realize—again—how visible the paralysis truly was! In a kind of twist of fate, he would become one of the few doctors there that I would get to know on a peer basis!

On another occasion as I was walking through the outpatient residence where out-of-town patients stayed while on some kind of therapy, an elderly lady on radiation treatment saw me and noticed the paralysis.

"You're one of us!" she exclaimed.

"No, I don't have cancer," I told her. "I had polio when I was a child."

However, her observation was a fascinating one, a learning experience for me. She apparently believed that since I, too, must have cancer, that I could better identify with and understand persons like her and what they were going through than could the "normal," healthy staff person!

POLIO

Several years later (1982–1983), while my wife, Jena, and son, Daryl, and I were living in Wichita, Kansas, in addition to my hospital chaplaincy work at the VA medical center, I took on the job of a part-time pastor of a small congregation in Udall, a small town near Wichita. As I was later told, one of the church members had informed the church governing board that she believed that, because of my facial paralysis, I should not be allowed to preach there, that it would be too much of a distraction. Interestingly, there IS a kind of biblical precedent for this. In the rules and regulations of Leviticus, we hear the Lord telling Moses to say to Aaron:

> ... For no one who has a blemish shall draw near (to offer the food of his God), one who is blind or lame, or one who has a mutilated face or a limb too long, or a man who has a broken foot or a broken hand, or a hunchback.... (Leviticus 21:18–20)[9]

Ironically, several months later, one of this family's daughters became chronically ill, and of all the church families, I suspect that this family appreciated my pastoral care the most! In their appreciation for my being with them in their time of need, they gave me a rare, out-of-print book, *Four Years in Paradise* by Osa Johnson, the traveling companion of Martin Johnson, early explorers of Africa.

In April of 1990, when I was forty-eight years old, I had another one of those "encounters" while attending one of my son's soccer games. As I sat in the bleachers, waiting for the game to start, I noticed one of the players of the other team (probably eleven or twelve years old) imitating my facial paralysis to some of his friends and pointing at me. I felt little less than fury! "Not *this* again!" My gut reaction was to want to lash out! I wanted to go over and shake the little "brat" and try to tell him what it is all about; but he wouldn't have listened. I doubt that he would have understood. But then, I'm not sure that a lot of people *want* to understand the person living with some kind of visible physical anomaly. I suspect that many of us want to be able to point at others' "inferior human status" so that we can feel better about ourselves. Perhaps this dynamic is the foundation of racism and sexism, and all of the other "isms?"

One day in 1991, as I checked out at a local grocery store, I noticed a teenage boy staring at me and grinning. Then, as we walked out of the store, he deliberately urged his friend to (take a) look at me. Again, the STRONG feelings: murder or suicide? Since neither seems to be a satisfactory option, I find that I have to do some extremely quick mental work:

- Consider the source.
- Forgive and forget.
- Go about your business as if nothing has happened.
- He doesn't know better.

But one is still wounded, still hurt. There is more, still more hemorrhaging of one's "existential energy"!

I am also aware, from time to time, that someone, especially children, will often move around in front of me to get a better look at my face: "There's something wrong with your face. Let me take a closer look. You are different; not normal." One little girl looked up at me and said: "Your mouth is upside down."

Two young boys (four to six years old) at a fast-food restaurant started staring at me, and when their older sister returned, encouraged her to "look at that man over there." Embarrassed, she awkwardly told them to turn around and eat. Again, it was another reminder that the facial paralysis is very visible.

On another occasion, when I was shopping at a local grocery store (I seem to spend a great deal of time in grocery stores!), a young girl, about five or six years old who noticed my facial paralysis was obviously stunned by what she had seen. She actually followed me down the aisle for twenty or twenty-five feet, staring at my face. She seemed not to see me as a thinking, feeling, conscious human being; so, for her, it was okay to stare at me. I realize that a child of that age has not yet developed a self-awareness of how she comes across to others, that she is not at all self-conscious about staring, but is simply interested and intrigued. Nevertheless, not only did I feel a sense of irritation, but I also felt a sense of surprise; surprised that the facial anomaly was so obvious: at a glance, the young girl saw the "difference." It was another "encounter of the uncomfortable kind."

One day, when my son was in the fifth grade, he reluctantly informed me that he didn't want me to go with him into his classroom because it embarrassed him. Some of the other students, he said, thought that I was "weird" because of my facial paralysis! I think I now know why, in the past, people with some kind of visible physical anomaly were often shunted off to the "back room" of the house to be kept out of sight!

Occasionally, when I see a horror movie (which is very seldom) in which the "creature" or the murderer has some kind of facial deformity, I find myself wondering how others around me are thinking; and if they are thinking of my facial paralysis.

I have a tendency to become so caught up in my daily activities, which is normal, that I forget about my facial paralysis and how it is on public display and viewed by others; until I notice someone staring at me in one of those "encounters of the uncomfortable kind" that I have shared. Children are especially good at this, but adults occasionally also bring it to my attention. One patient commented:

"You must have been injured."

Another one:

"You can't talk very well."

Once, as I stepped into a hospital room to visit a patient, a patient I had visited on several other occasions, I was jolted by his comment:

"What happened to you? You have a tooth pulled?"

This kind of largely innocent "reminding" also happens when I encounter another person who also has a facial paralysis perhaps from a stroke (many people immediately assume that this is what I had), Bell's palsy, or even another very rare bulbar polio survivor. In 2010 I met a woman, a Walmart greeter, who also had facial paralysis due to polio. I generated enough courage to speak to her and talk of our experiences.

Or I'm reminded all over again when I see myself in a photograph, or in a mirror.

Once, a VA nursing home resident, upon seeing me come down the hall to conduct a short service, commented to another resident:

– "Here comes the chaplain, the one with the hare-lip."

From such remarks, it can be seen that a person becomes identified by the visible physical anomaly:

"He's the chaplain with the crooked mouth."

"He's the kid with the weird smile."

Because of such painful encounters during the years following polio (of course, as I noted before, there is no such thing as "following polio" or "after polio" if one has been permanently paralyzed in some way. Its residual effects become a constant, life-long companion!), I began consciously to realize that I had some very difficult decisions to make in life, decisions about relationships, and about how I understood myself:

– How do I handle people who make fun of my facial paralysis?
– How do I handle questioning stares?
– Do I ignore them, as if I'm unaware of their stares?
– Do I speak to them?

(This latter reaction has brought about some amusing reactions, especially from children. To speak to the staring person often catches her or him off guard, and the person will quickly look and walk away, at times not even returning my acknowledgment. Perhaps the person does not feel the need to return my acknowledgment because he/she does not feel that I am human enough; or perhaps I have "turned the tables," and suddenly that person felt awkwardly self-conscious?)

How do I handle apparent rejection of me as a human being solely because of my facial paralysis? But, then, how do I know when I am being rejected because of my facial paralysis, and not for some other reason?"

How do I handle my own feelings about myself and what has happened to me?

These were questions (I call this the "reaction dilemma") that I would confront and wrestle with again and again—questions that I have to answer at times, not very successfully, creatively, or redemptively! In this inner turmoil, there seemed (and seems!) to be somewhat of a choice. I could either withdraw from as many social contacts as possible and establish an introverted lifestyle which, at times, seemed (and seems) a very seductive option, or to stay "out there" in society even at the risk of being ridiculed and rejected and resolve to educate and sensitize people when they do. This tension still exists!

Interestingly, in about 1977, a seminary-contracted "Readiness for Ministry" psychologist, as a beneficially required part of our seminary education, indicated to me that he was surprised that I would choose to go into a profession (the ministry) which dealt so much with the public; that with my facial paralysis, I would have attempted to avoid public contact as much as possible! He was touching on the very struggles that I had been dealing with for years!

However, I have to thank my immediate and extended family for NOT hiding me in some dark backroom and keeping me from public contact. Instead, they saw beyond the paralysis and expected and encouraged me to "be all that I could be!"

In this, I must admit that I have had (and continue) to struggle with such potent feelings as anger, bitterness, frustration, depression, resignation, shame, and inferiority in my relationship to myself and toward others. Thus, such "Christian" concepts as forgiveness, patience, understanding, forbearance, and individual worth began to take on added significance and urgency after I had polio. These concepts moved from the abstract of the Sunday School Quarterly and the pulpit sermon, into the trenches of my everyday existence early on in my life. I now realize that I was being forced to put them into practice long before I "heard" about them in church settings! Further, the idea of God unconditionally loving all of us, no matter what, takes on greater urgency and significance!

These many and varied "encounters of the uncomfortable kind" have taught me that my facial paralysis is the first thing that people notice about me, thus often when I speak before a group of people, such as conducting a church service, I find it appropriate to give a little bit of my personal background, including the fact that as a child I had polio, which caused the facial paralysis. This answers their unasked questions and tends to put them at ease, plus many times they have stories of polio that they share.

I wonder from time to time what others—even friends—are *really* saying about me "behind my back" when I'm not around. Do they laugh and mimic my paralysis? Do they take me seriously or say:

"Oh, he's just a cripple."

"He'll take anything I offer."

"You can't expect too much from him."

And what about the friendly people? What do they *really* think? If in a moment of anger, they lash out at my paralysis, is that attitude underlying their friendliness:

"As long as you know your place, you cripple, and you stay in it; we'll treat you nicely, but if you attempt to feel that you are as good as we are, we'll have to slap you down."

There is also the problem of becoming overly self-conscious or too sensitive. One can begin to feel that in order to compensate for the anomaly and how one believes others perceive him/her, one must act and behave perfectly. Any mistake will surely be seen by others as being caused by or, in some way, connected to the anomaly, or as Erving Goffman said:

> …during mixed contacts, the stigmatized individual is likely to feel that he is "on," having to be self-conscious and calculating about the impression he is making, to a degree and in areas of conduct which he assumes others are not.
>
> …
>
> …minor failings or incidental impropriety may, he feels, be interpreted as a direct expression of his stigmatized differentness.[10]

The convoluted thinking then takes over:

− Am I <u>too</u> sensitive?
− Am I making a mountain out of a mole hill?"
− Am I too thin-skinned?"

This "border-line paranoia" extends even to friends and acquaintances in small, fleeting incidents:

Is she or is she not, is he or is he not mimicking my facial paralysis?

This can also happen when I meet a fellow co-worker in public out on the street or in a store, and the person fails to acknowledge my presence:

− Is he/she too embarrassed about me to let others know that he/she knows me?

At times, I wonder if "normals" praise those with visible physical anomalies, when the VPAs keep quiet, because "normals" cannot, or do not want to, handle the realities that VPAs have to deal with. For instance, a person is labeled a "complainer," a "wimp," or one who can't cope if that VPA attempts to be honest and "tell it like it is." "Normals" praise those who do not bother them with the reality of the struggle: they want VPAs to struggle in silence(?). Related to this, a 1992 conversation with a paraplegic at a V.A medical center made me suspect that "normals" use the derogatory term "pity-pot" to keep those with physical anomalies or disabilities from sharing what they <u>really</u> have to deal with in their daily lives. "Normals" like to pretend that the disabled has heroically overcome any difficulties and has moved on with a normal life; or, that the disabled should stoically deny any hardship or discrimination or continuing struggle.

As I was traveling through the dating years, I often wondered if a girl who "dropped" me was doing so because of my facial paralysis. On the other hand, if a girl *did* go out with me, was she doing it because she was really interested in me as a person, or because she felt sorry for me! Even when I interviewed for a position and was rejected, I wondered if part of that rejection was due to the facial paralysis. On the other hand: "Did I get this job because someone felt sorry for me?" In this, one can become a "borderline paranoid": do they or don't they; is it or isn't it a fact? It becomes a game of psychological "daisy-petal-picking"! Erving Goffman noted that

> ...in the stigmatized arises the sense of not knowing what the others present are 'really' thinking about him.[11]

There is a kind of irony in all of this: a differentness or physical anomaly which may keep people from hiring me for a pastoral care position may, in reality, make me a better pastoral care provider than a more "hirable" normal person who does not have an anomaly. That "normal" may be less able to appreciate or empathize with the hurts of other people!

At times I wonder if having had polio at such an early age (eleven years old) was better than having contracted it later in life. I was able to "grow up with it" and was able to integrate it into my emerging lifestyle, self-image, and value system, whereas older persons who suddenly face some kind of disability or anomaly are already "set in their ways" and thus find it hard to adjust(?). At the age of eleven I was just becoming aware of life and was in the process of forming values, priorities, goals, and world views. In a sense, I was still flexible or pliable in my understanding of self and reality; thus, I was, early on, able to start incorporating and integrating the fact of facial paralysis into the way I saw and understood life and the human condition.

Early in life I would begin to see that life is not necessarily a "bowl of cherries"; that life *does* include some pretty hard knocks and bumpy roads along the way; that life is *not* easy and smooth; that we do not play on a level playing field and that life is "unfair." Early on, perhaps before most young people my age, I learned what Harvey Potthoff, my theology professor in seminary wrote:

> … No person lives under ideal circumstances. Life is offered to each individual on different terms. Life comes to mean somewhat different things to different persons. Yet, each human being can seek such fulfillment as is possible and appropriate to his situation. It is not a matter of having everything or nothing. Life is the art of the possible. To seek the possibilities in each situation for sensitive, appreciative, creative living is to seek the way of life fulfillment and celebration.[12]

Somewhat related to this, I wonder if many persons who incur disabilities or physical anomalies later in life have already, for so many years, looked down on such persons as inferior beings, so that when they themselves go through that experience, it is shaming and psycho-spiritually crushing? In this, Beatrice Wright has observed,

> …so long as a physically able person links disability with shame, he or she will be ill prepared for the challenge of living with a disability that may come with time.[13]

As we all struggle to feel good about ourselves—struggle to feel that our personal existence has legitimacy…struggle to establish and maintain a certain amount of self-esteem— we tend to put others down. By making someone else or some other group inferior to us, we can feel better about ourselves. Persons with physical disabilities or visible physical anomalies are perfect targets: "Obviously, they are not as good as we are!" Again, Wright:

> …as long as the attacker needs someone to step on to sustain his or her own uncertain status, the abuse will continue until the desired response of suffering is elicited. … The bully must get the unfortunate person to admit the superiority of the attacker.
> … The bully seeks another scapegoat because defeat at the hands of the first has injured a vulnerable self-esteem still further, an insult that can be avenged by forcing inferiority on someone else.
> …
> …the need to tear another person down in order to build oneself up…. The bully, too, is a person with a disability, in this case an emotional disability….[14]

The book, *Twenty-Four Hours a Day*, a book of daily readings for alcoholics, observes:

> I used to run people down all the time. I realize now that it was because I wanted unconsciously to build myself up.[15]

And yet, there are times, when in my convoluted thinking, I wonder if "they" *are* right: that we who have physical anomalies and disabilities *are* inferior human beings—less than "normal"—and that all of these intellectual/psychological/spiritual/mental gymnastics that we do are only frantic attempts to feel legitimate and worthwhile.

I suspect that a VPA has to develop a very strong sense of self-worth and human (existential) legitimacy to creatively counter the pressure to feel inferior. But, then, perhaps I am supposed to be ashamed of the paralysis? Perhaps I *should* withdraw into seclusion so that the public doesn't have to confront reality? From time to time, I read a story or hear an account of someone who would rather die than be physically scarred for life, as if death would be preferable to being a VPA. I once ministered to a professional woman who said, at the time, that she would rather die of cancer than to have a mastectomy.

Thinking about age and incurring a disability, I become very angry when I read or hear about or see something about some young adult who recently became facially disfigured, perhaps through war, and how brave and courageous that person is to go on living with such a horrible trauma! What in the world do they think that I and many others have been doing for many, many years?! At times, I suspect that the people, who are around me often and are "used to" my paralysis, don't notice it and assume that I have learned to handle or accept it well…that I don't struggle with it…and that *I* do not need to be brave or courageous to live with my situation. I have trouble with statements like: "I admire your courage and strength in handling this handicap." What does this mean? What else can one do but keep on keeping on? I've never considered myself "strong" or "courageous" or as one possessing "great faith" or having a "strong belief" in God.

Actually, when it comes to belief in God, I am somewhat of a skeptic or agnostic. Sometimes I wonder if all this talk about "God" is just an effort to cope with reality. Do we create an all-powerful "god" to deal with that over which we have no control, such as death; an all-loving god to deal with our need to be loved; and a god of judgment to punish those whom we feel have wronged us in some way (or as a fellow seminary student observed: "Heaven wouldn't be heavenly if there were not a hell for those we don't like!")!?

And then there is the line: "God is good." What does this mean? In what way or ways is God "good?" Why should I, who have experienced permanent partial facial paralysis due to polio, with all of its attendant consequences, believe that God is "good?"

And "courage." Is this a term used by "normals" to make the disabled or "different" feel good? Further, as far as strength and courage and faith go, there have been many times when I have gone to bed at night hoping not to have to wake up the next morning to face another painful, seemingly meaningless day! But then perhaps these kinds of experiences have helped me be more empathetic with others who have gone through the same thing?

If a VPA/handicapped person starts to share his/her authentic fears, pain, frustrations, etc., he/she is just "complaining," a "whinny baby."

The best way to shut such a person down—and thus further isolate him/her—is to tell him/her that she/he is a chronic complainer or that he/she shouldn't feel that way. Yet, to deny one's personal struggles will keep a person from being able to help others. To deny or suppress their feelings will keep them from appreciating the feelings of others who face crises. To deny one's own personal experience will keep a person from effectively ministering to others.

Every now and then we also hear a story of how a person has "overcome" some handicap, a person who, we find out, was already a doctor or a talented artist or a star athlete or an actor. In other words, he or she is a person who had already developed skills and abilities—as well as finances and influence and fame—which could be used even in the midst of a physical handicap. Or that the person was "well-heeled" financially so that she/he could afford special treatment and education and equipment necessary to overcome the handicap. And we marvel and become teary eyed. However, not all people who struggle with handicaps or visible physical anomalies are born with "silver spoons" in their mouths. Some are born into and live in homes of very modest means, in less-than-loving homes. Thus, to point to the privileged or extremely talented person as an example to emulate and to look up to is dangerous in that it can make the handicapped person feel guilty and worthless: failure to measure up because he/she cannot "paint with her/his toes!" In this, I very much appreciate the observation of Leonard Bowman:

> Despite the success stories, hero stories, and examples of what is possible for the handicapped person, the more common story is one of struggle, repeated frustration, and shattered self-respect.[16]

Further, while many who have or acquire some form of disability or VPA live among persons who are supportive, accepting, encouraging, and caring (as I was), others live in very different kinds of relationship environments in which there is no support, acceptance, love, or encouragement. This has a great impact upon how the "different" person develops! To feel that one is unloved, and even worse, unlovable, can be devastating to a person…ANY person!

I think that one of the greatest struggles of the person with a visible physical anomaly is the sense of helplessness in the face of ridicule. One realizes that those who are ridiculing one's anomaly are technically "right" in that the person *is* different.

This "differentness" can lead to what I call "specialness" that is often attached to those who have visible physical anomalies. First, a person with anomalies may be seen by some as being morally or spiritually above or superior to the common person…as a person who "knows" what suffering is all about, and thus can somehow empathize with others who are suffering.

For example, one Christmas while I was home on vacation, I visited an acquaintance who had cancer. During the conversation, she indicated that with all that I had been through with my polio, I could better understand what she was going through than could others. Further, as I worked among hospital patients, there were times when I perceived that they "appreciated" my polio experience in that because of it, I could better relate to their own struggles, and that I couldn't be too arrogant because I, too, was "afflicted."

A variation on this theme is that there are those who believe that God "knew" that we had enough faith to handle such a burden, and thus we are a "cut above" everyone else...almost saintly! Let me quickly state that I am no saint! That would be a very hard image for me to live out!

Another variation is the idea that we are bearing our cross *now*; thus, there is a special place in "heaven" for us!

On the opposite end of the spectrum, there are others who view a person with some kind of visible anomaly as radically different: as being morally flawed or impure ("morally handicapped"): "He/she must have done something terribly wrong to deserve this kind of punishment!" They feel that the person must be paying for some kind of sin she/he has committed; that God is punishing them. Hugh Gregory Gallagher, in his book about Franklin Roosevelt's struggle with polio, observed that up until recently,

> ... In a very real although subconsciously motivated sense, the handicapped were viewed as flawed in moral character as well as in body. The physical handicap was, as it were, an outward sign of some inner weakness! It was widely held that treatment, to be effective, must have a punitive quality to it. Those who administered this painful treatment did so in fulfillment of their Christian duty, in answer to their calling to a life of Christian service.[17]

Related to the "morally handicapped" (and the borderline paranoia) dilemma(s) is the idea that such people are not to be trusted. They may even be seen as a part of the "criminal element": perverse, degenerate, immoral, e.g., the Elephant Man, the Hunchback of Notre Dame, etc. Beatrice Wright has pointed to three such references.[18]

> It has been stated that the nondisabled unconsciously believe that the cripple has committed some evil act and is therefore dangerous; or, if he has not done so, that he will do something wrong in order to warrant his punishment (Meng, 1938;[19] reported in Barker et al.,

> 1953, p. 87[20]). That evil acts are associated with marked physical deviation has been shown in an experiment in which nondisfigured persons reacted to photographs of persons with facial anomalies. ... The investigators concluded that "facial features which served as false clues led respondents not only to impute to these patients personality traits considered socially unacceptable, but to assign them roles and statuses on an inferior social level". ... In the same study, a patient with a disfigured face resulting from war injuries recounted, "When I parked my car in front of a jewelry store, two cops came up and asked me for my identification card. They thought I was a gangster." Magregor et al., 1953[21]

Occasionally, when I am in a store and I notice (or at least *think* that I notice) a clerk eyeing me suspiciously, I wonder if he/she is doing so because of my facial paralysis: "Here's a weird-looking guy who is not to be trusted!" I must admit that, at times, I feel like jumping out at the individual and shouting, "Boo!"

Thirdly, the person with the anomaly may be seen by some as one who must be "taken care of"..."protected"...treated with "kid gloves"... or pampered as if the person is unusually fragile, which is a form of condescension. Further, this "crippled" person need not be taken too seriously. She/he is a person who should be humored along to make him/her feel like a real part of the normal human race ("...even though *we* know he/she really isn't"). Erving Goffman reflects that

> ... By definition, of course, we believe the person with a stigma is not quite human. On this assumption we exercise varieties of discrimination, through which we effectively, if often unthinkingly, reduce his life chances. We construct a stigma-theory, an ideology to explain his inferiority and account for the danger he represents, sometimes rationalizing an animosity based on other differences, such as those of social class. ... We tend to impute a wide range of imperfections on the basis of the

> original one, and at the same time to impute some desirable but undesired attributes, often of a supernatural cast, such as 'sixth sense,' or 'understanding'....[22]

There are certain fallacies that I encounter among people. First, there is the soothing saying: "Everyone is handicapped in some way." People will occasionally say this to me, perhaps in an effort to make me feel less alone, or to feel better about my paralysis? One of my favorite theology professors in seminary used to say this from time to time; and, in a sense, he is correct. We are ALL either morally, spiritually, physically, mentally, or intellectually handicapped. However, not all handicaps are equal! And I find that often the person who says something like this usually does *not* have some kind of visible physical difference!

The second fallacy I encounter is, "You are lucky that more things aren't wrong with you!" Again, I suppose that this is to make one feel better...to feel lucky or blessed; however, it is a great "guilt trip!" Well, of course, I'm fortunate that I did not end up in an iron lung or with more physical disabilities. However, could I not have been lucky enough or blessed enough or fortunate enough *not* to have had polio in the first place?! I assume that such statements are made by "normals" who don't know what else to say and are apparently attempting to make me feel good about my experience. A variation of this theme is something like, "God was really watching over you that you survived polio," or, "Aren't you glad that God protected you from further disability." My mental, if not verbal, response to this: "Well, if God is in the protection business, why didn't God protect me from polio in the first place?!" Of course, this experience taught me, early on in life, that God is *not* "the Great Cosmic Protector." Even the most devout persons are vulnerable to the pain of the human condition!

There is a kind of "intellectual dishonesty," conscious or unconscious, in statements like these. To be intellectually honest, one must *also* be willing to go the other direction, that is, if one is *lucky* that

God was watching out for him, then it also must be stated that he/she is *unlucky* to have contracted polio in the first place.

It is similar to the oft stated observation by patients: "When I look around, I see people *much worse* off than I am"—to which, one could rejoin: "Well, when you look around, you also see people *much better* off than you!" Sometimes, I suspect that such statements are made to create a certain amount of guilt—and shame?—in the afflicted person.

I think that one should realize that while nowadays there are all kinds of support groups for persons struggling with various issues, and a growing awareness of the psycho-spiritual dimension of physical handicaps and anomalies, in the 1950s there was no such thing, at least in the area in which I lived. One supposedly "recovered" from the illness and went on with his/her life as if nothing had happened, or was placed on the back burner of life.

Gradually, gently, quietly, in the midst of normal conversations with people among whom I grew up, what they thought of me and my polio experience began coming forth. In the summer of 1992, a long-time resident of the Wall, Texas, community, in speaking to me of his own struggle against feeling sorry for himself, added something like: "…as you probably felt after you had polio."

From time to time over the past years, I have wondered how things "might have been" if I had not had polio and the consequent facial paralysis. One of the things that I was extremely interested in while growing up was flying. I wanted to be an Air Force pilot. I was, and am, a great collector and have an insatiable thirst to learn all I can about a subject I am interested in. Therefore, as I was growing up, I sent out a constant stream of letters of inquiry to aircraft manufacturers and to Air Force installations. I'm surprised that at some point the FBI didn't come out to our farm to investigate! I set my sights on the Air Force.

However, in another one of those "psycho-spiritual" blows that are part of having a visible physical anomaly, I found that because of the paralysis, the Air Force would not accept me for pilot training. After years of hope and planning, I had to struggle to pick up the pieces, divert my energies elsewhere, and go on. It was a time of reorientation and a time of "re-self-defining":

- Who am I?
- Where do I fit in?
- What if I had been accepted into pilot training, had become a pilot, and then had spent twenty to thirty years in the Air Force?

Instead, I went into Army ROTC (1960–1964) with the idea of making the Army a career. The idea of "serving" was important to me.
REFLECTIONS (written by me several years ago):
The idea…the desire to…"serve", I suspect grows out of my being in touch with my own inner pain and struggles. Out of the awareness of my own woundedness, I wanted (want) to reach out and in some (very human) way, make life a little more livable for others.

I can remember vividly an occasion in high school when some kind of "extra-curricular" party was planned. I knew of some students who were not going to be able to be there, and I felt that I needed to be with them…with those who don't get to go to the parties of life…with those who are weeping while others are rejoicing.

Many years later, while I was involved in Clinical Pastoral Education (CPE) at M. D. Anderson Hospital in Houston, Texas, I was jolted by the memory of that high school occasion when, on a Christmas Eve, instead of being with my family, I chose to spend some time with a father and his young dying daughter in the hospital. Somehow, I felt I "belonged" there. And, perhaps that is what attracts me to the hospital chaplaincy: the need to be with those who are not at the parties of life.

However, when I took the Advanced Army ROTC physical exam, I was told that because of my facial paralysis, I could not become an

Army officer. That did it: I became extremely angry!

REFLECTIONS:

Anger, by the way, can be a potent, positive, creative motivating force in life. In this case, it was the motivating force behind my drive to receive my Army commission.

At another point in my life, I was madly in love with a beautiful young lady to whom I was convinced I would be married; until she informed me that she was going to marry someone else. My life fell into nothingness. I felt meaningless…useless…worthless…rejected…old…alone; and perhaps worst of all, bewildered and confused: "I thought I was doing God's will. If I am not, then how will I ever know when I <u>am</u> doing as God would want me to do? Why did this happen? Am I a failure at life? Can't anything in life work out like we would like it to? Why is life filled with such heartache and loneliness? There must be some reason…some purpose…for this kind of suffering and pain! If there is no meaning, if there is no ultimate purpose to pain and suffering, then is life worth living? What is one to expect out of life?" As I struggled between the desire to go to sleep and never wake up and the desire to keep on keeping on, I began to feel angry…<u>very</u> angry: "God, I don't know what you are doing, but I am <u>not</u> going to be pulled under by this horrible experience. I am <u>not</u> going to be defeated in this "game" of life!" I verbally shook my fist at God…at "fate"…at pain and suffering…at misfortune…at, at whatever! I was defiant! I was tired of hurting, and I wasn't going to take it any longer! It was the energy generated by this anger that pushed me…drove me…into seminary: not because I believed that I had found "the answer," but because I was defiantly looking for some answers!

In the case of ROTC, I sat down and composed a letter to the Commanding General of the Fourth Army Area in which my ROTC unit was located. I could see no earthly reason why my facial paralysis would keep me from being an Army officer! He offered me the option of having a civilian neurologist examine me or going to an Army doctor to see if the particular regulation could be waived. I chose a civilian doctor in Lubbock, Texas, who could not understand why the Army was making such a big deal out of such a (to him) minor thing. With his report, I was allowed into Advanced ROTC and eventually received a Commission. I would serve as an Army officer for four years, one of which was in Viet Nam. My sense of serving was so strong that I requested to be sent to Viet Nam. I believed that all career-minded officers should request to be sent into combat zones: that's what they are/were paid and trained for.

This particular episode in my life raises an interesting question: Did I pursue the military career because I was really interested in that kind of lifestyle, or because of the challenge of being told that because of the facial paralysis I could not do it? While I think that I did it because of a genuine personal interest (and I continue to be interested in national security affairs and foreign policy), the question is still intriguing: Do we, whether "handicapped" or not, need some kind of challenge…an "enemy"…an "adversary," in order to be motivated in life? Do we need something or someone to be up "against"…someone or something we can vent our anger toward and blame for all of our troubles? Do we need something or someone to be "against" in order to develop a sense of personal or corporate identity? Erik Erikson wrote:

> It is easy enough and, up to a point, necessary for leaders to offer youth, as well as to the perennial adolescent in adults, some overdefined enemies *against whom* to maintain a sense of identity.[23]

Or do we need something or someone to be "against" in order to be morally good as in the threat of eternal punishment, the "devil," and hell? Does having an "adversary" help generate a kind of energy...give us a reason for being...give us a "cause" to be for...give us a team to be on...give us an identity?

And, perhaps a step further in this process of thinking: Do I really, truly want to be physically healed of this paralysis; or does it give me a unique identity...give me an "adversary"...give me something to be over against, and an excuse when things aren't going right? Erving Goffman has said:

> The stigmatized individual is likely to use his stigma for "secondary gains," as an excuse for ill success that has come his way for other reasons....[24]

And he points to Baker and Smith's insight:

> When one removes this factor (the stigma) by surgical repair, the patient is cast adrift from the more or less acceptable emotional protection it has offered and soon he finds, to his surprise and discomfort, that life is not all smooth sailing even for those with unblemished, 'ordinary' faces. He is unprepared to cope with this situation without the support of a "handicap,"....[25]

Is the paralysis something I can blame for my troubles...my failures and defeats? I often wonder how I would react if I were told that the paralysis could be "fixed"!

And, in come the "doctors"...the healers! A person that has some kind of visible physical anomaly is going to be the target of many who "have the answer"...those who know of some cure to the problem. I have encountered them. When I was in the Army, an enlisted man insisted that a spice named "Gloves," placed on the paralyzed portion of my face over a several-day period, could heal the paralysis! Another person assured me that it could be "fixed," but he did not know how.

Was he trying to give me hope that somehow, I could be returned to being "normal?"

On the more legitimate side, when I was working in the Defense Intelligence Agency in Washington, DC, one of my fellow analysts brought a magazine article to the office one day that dealt with advances in neurosurgery which could repair such things. I appreciated this interest, and did follow up the article with a visit to a local neurologist, who happened to know the people mentioned in the article. He was not optimistic, but he did show me what limited things could be done.

When I was a student at Iliff School of Theology in Denver in the mid-1970s, I took a course entitled "Theology & Psychiatry in Dialogue." The psychiatrist involved with teaching the course noticed my paralysis, felt that perhaps something could be done about it, and requested my old medical records (see Appendix). He wanted to see if, indeed, it was really polio. Fascinatingly, I was able, with the help of my mother, to obtain a copy of those records, which by then were over twenty-five years old! He had a neurologist examine them and conclude that, indeed, I had had polio and that the paralysis was permanent.

In 2009, while my father-in-law was struggling with serious, and terminal, illness in a Denver hospital, a neurosurgeon noticed my facial paralysis as I sat innocently in a hospital hallway. He did an "about-face" and told me that perhaps he could correct the paralysis. Sometime later, I made an appointment with him, and he graciously went over several options, none of which, to be honest, attracted me. However, he came the closest to offering some legitimate "hope."

I have to wonder if my sense of humor, at times rather bizarre, has something to do with attempting to cope with the paralysis. Have I evolved a sense of humor as a way to break down barriers to communication…to put others, or myself, at ease…to ease the tension I perceive in others at first contact? Is it a way to help others get past or beyond my facial paralysis? Is it a way to deal with my own anger? Or is it a way to keep others at a distance?

At the same time, I can easily swing into periods of depression, melancholy, reverie, or a kind of sadness at what I see as the tragic aspects of life. One person once observed: "Your pain makes you keenly aware of the pain inherent in life, all around." This may be the reason why I am attracted to some of the heavier, more somber classical music. To me, it reflects the tragedy of human existence; yet it also contains various strains which seem to represent or symbolize the struggle of the human spirit to overcome the tragedies.

As I mentioned earlier, one does not "get over" a permanent physical anomaly. It is a part of the reality of everyday life. And one must deal with it, even to the point of personal "existential exhaustion": the grinding down of one's soul...the wearing away at one's will to go on. It can be like a psycho-spiritual cancer which eats away at one's desire to live. It is not as if it were a single mountain or obstacle which can be overcome once and for all, then to be followed by gentle flat lands and rolling prairies for the remainder of the journey. It is a continuing series of mountain ranges which must be climbed...surmounted.

If one goes up into the foothills of the Rockies just south and west of Denver, there is a place called Devil's Head. Looking toward the east from that vantage point, one sees the broad expanse of the high plains disappearing into the haze. If one turns and faces west, one sees a whole series of mountain ranges shading into various shades of purple.

I would like to suggest that life is more like the journey through the mountains than over the plains: a series of mountain ranges, of various heights and difficulties, to be surmounted. The sooner we understand life this way, the better we will be able to cope with the journey ahead. All too often, I suspect, we feel that if we can just overcome one more obstacle (mountain) we will be out on the open prairie with easy traveling for the rest of the way; and when, upon reaching the summit of the mountain, we look ahead, and see, not plains, but more mountains, we become disillusioned and may even feel deceived ("This is *not* the way it's supposed to be!")

Most of the time, overcoming one mountain gives us a kind of reassurance that we can also overcome future mountains: overcoming one builds confidence for the next one. However, I must admit that there are times when, looking over the mountain ranges ahead, I have wondered if it is really worth the effort. As Hugh G. Gallagher noted:

> ... This condition of being handicapped generates a range of emotions, whether expressed or not, that must be dealt with, not just at onset, but continuing throughout the rest of the patient's life.[26]

Further physical deterioration, whether or not it is related to the original anomaly, can cause renewed discouragement:

What else can go wrong?

What's the use of fighting anymore? There's a sense of being whipped at last; licked; finally beaten. There are just too many new mountains to be climbed.

I would suggest that what helps us to "keep on keeping on" as we encounter the various mountain ranges of life is *love: being and feeling loved, feeling lovable, and having someone to love*. I became acutely aware of this need to be loved and lovable when working with psychiatric patients as a chaplain. Many of them spoke of feeling unloved and unlovable, especially when they were growing up; and they found a sense of being accepted, loved, and cared for right there in the psychiatric program. They said that they felt for the first time in their lives, somebody cared for them.

One day, when I walked into the classroom for my "Life Journey Challenges" class that I was teaching there in the VA psych unit, I noticed one of the female patients looking at a small paperback book. I asked her what she was looking at, and she showed me Eugene Kennedy's book, *If You Really Knew Me Would You Still Like Me?* (1975). I asked her what it was *about* the book that attracted her. As she shared, our conversation began to ripple through others in the group, and the subject of loving took off. (The topic I had originally planned to talk about was forgotten!) At the beginning of Eugene Kennedy's book are found such truths as:

> ...although pride and arrogance are called the big sins of the age, most people die of the little ones of self-doubt and insecurity. Too many of us are saying, "I don't see what anybody else could see in me, not if they looked close anyway, not if they knew what I know about myself." Many think not too well but too ill of themselves; they are not overbearing as much as they are underconfident. The bravest of public postures may, after all, mask a private trembling and unsure heart.
> ...
> Is there a crueler dilemma than that which faces the underconfident? They want to be close, but that opens them to rejection if others get a good look at them; they pull back to spare themselves the wounds of intimacy and thereby intensify their loneliness.
> ...
> ... To feel alive they must feel loved. They must sense that somebody else notices and makes room for them, that they measure up in the eyes of somebody else who likes them just as they are.
> ...
> The great American pastime is not sports but the game of looking good and getting liked.[27]

I suspect that people with some kind of visible physical anomaly use up more psycho-spiritual energy in living life than do "normals." This energy is used up or needed to deal with trying to prove one's worth and ability and sanity: to show others that in spite of the "difference," one *can* do the job...that one *does* have talents and abilities...that one is *not* an inferior human being. This extra energy needed to live is a double-edged sword: it can strengthen one to better cope with life and life's frustrations; however, it can also exhaust a person, wearing down the will to go on...tearing away or eroding the will to fight the necessary battles which come with attempting to be all that that person can be…to work at what one does best.

There is "energy" used up just getting up in the morning, knowing that one will face more stares and insults and questions and demeaning statements and rejections and condescending attitudes…knowing that one will *again* have to work through some very strong feelings. Somewhere I read that the real heroes of life are not soldiers who face danger in battle only for a relatively short time, but are people with handicaps who get up each morning of their life ready to struggle each day!

There is also the problem of "spread" or "connection": "If he/she is physically impaired or different, then she/he must also be mentally, intellectually, emotionally, psychologically, spiritually, and even morally impaired or flawed!" There is the idea that if there is something physically "wrong" or different with a person, there *must* be something wrong with her/him in these other areas as well.

Two points grow out of this phenomenon. First, the person with the "differentness" may sooner or later begin to accept this idea of "spread" himself or herself; and thus it becomes a kind of self-fulfilling prophecy. This then adds to the "handicapping" condition of the "differentness," because the person's sense of self-worth begins to descend into the abyss.

Secondly, and paradoxically, because of the struggle with "differentness" the person *is* often going to develop or evolve a different outlook on life; different goals, priorities, and values; a different way of seeing things than the "normal" person, and thus *may* indeed come across as being different or "weird" in his/her thinking! The person, through intellectual struggles, *may* indeed leave the mainstream of social, philosophical, theological thought, values, goals, and priorities, and move into other realms in order to cope with and to make sense out of his or her "differentness." He/she is forced to take another look at the assumed answers that others take for granted. Those answers no longer fit the reality that the "different" person experiences.

A further observation about the problem of "spread" is that many actions, ideas, and opinions (which may, in fact, be totally unrelated to the visible physical anomaly) of such a person are often excused or dismissed by others as being a part of or a result of the anomaly.

I often wonder if there is much more "pressure" on the person with the physical anomaly to deal with and, if possible, to answer some of the tougher questions of life than there is pressure on the so-called "normal" person:

- Why did this happen to <u>me</u>?
- What does it mean, in the face of such a problem, to be human?
- How will I live out my life in the face of such an anomaly?
- Is life worth living with such an anomaly?
- Who am I; and how do I identify myself?
- Why is there suffering in life?
- What are some values and priorities one can live with which can transcend this anomaly?

I suspect that I was forced to begin dealing with these kinds of questions long before my peers did. For many of them, the process of growing up was "normal"; for me, it was not. Perhaps this is what people are trying to say when they speak of a young person being "mature beyond her/his years": that person has been forced to deal with philosophical or theological questions which most people don't encounter or struggle with until much later in life, if ever. Perhaps the polio forced me to realize that life is *not* neat and orderly; forced me to question the idea that "good" people are exempt from or protected (by God) from suffering; forced me to question the idea that "everything always works out for the best." It doesn't. As Leonard Bowman has said,

> ...Sickness forces the sick person to come to terms with the reality of the human condition, and through him confronts our society with a sign of contradiction, a challenge to truth.

> It is quite easy to avoid that truth. We tend to skate merrily along like water bugs on the thin, deceptive surface of living, and never think to let ourselves be immersed in its depth. Until something disturbs that surface, at least – like sickness. Then the depths make their claim, and either a person learns to live more deeply or he drowns.
>
> Sickness suggests that living means more than the smooth surface. Living includes suffering pain, confronting the ugly and dealing with it honestly, and going through the bumps, frustrations and struggles that are part of the process of growth, change, and deepening. And this process goes on throughout life – so there is never a valid basis for a complacent sense of "having arrived."[28]

In other words, I learned early in life that there is often a difference between what one is taught about life and what one experiences in life.

Because of the polio experience, and the earlier experience of appendicitis, which I now know, many years later, almost killed me, my parents could no longer protect me from the "slings and arrows of outrageous fortune" as William Shakespeare put it in *Hamlet*, Act III, Scene I (*To be, or not to be*). Parents normally attempt to protect their children from some of the harsher aspects of life as long as possible; however, when a devastating illness or accident strikes a child, the parents can no longer hide the realities of life from that child. (Perhaps there is no greater sense of helplessness than for a parent to watch a child suffer.) The child, even with the help of others, then has to come to terms with those realities on his or her own.

As long as we don't encounter suffering and tragedy, or as long as we practice a kind of denial that we hurt (often for religious or cultural reasons), we have no need to call into question inherited ideas about life and the human condition, ideas that come from centuries and millennia of church and society. However, once we encounter the storms of life, and are willing to admit that they are indeed storms, then much of what we have been led to believe is called into question. Many of those "pat" answers no longer seem to fit reality as we experience it. They are no longer adequate to the task of being human. We begin to realize that what we have inherited is adequate as long as nothing bad happens to us; or as long as we can deny that anything bad has happened to us. We begin to realize that many of the shallow cliches and proverbs about life just don't fit.

Especially overcoming and struggling with the feeling of inferiority—which, to a certain extent exists within *all* human beings—was to become one of the greatest challenges of my life. In a very real sense, I became "driven" to prove my personal worth…to "justify my existence." But to whom? To myself? To others? To God? Perhaps to "all of the above?"

There is a certain "drivenness" within me which may be connected to the facial paralysis. This "drivenness" is especially manifested in my being a voracious reader, especially of philosophy, theology, biographies, anthropology, history, and psycho-social aspects of human existence. As I look back over my life, I often wonder if I was born with the propensity to be "philosophical," to wonder about things and to muse upon life. However, I also have to wonder if my philosophical/theological "bent" has been made more acute, more passionate and less dispassionate, more obsessive, and more necessary because of the facial paralysis.

Robert M. Baird suggests that personal meaning is not so much discovered or found as it is created:

> … to speak of creating a meaningful life suggests that we have a responsibility for its coming into being…
>
> Part of what it means, then, to be fully human is to create meaning by establishing depth relationships, by committing ourselves to projects that give order and purpose to our days, and by placing our lives in the context of meaning-creating stories.[29]

I suspect that the search for meaning or, perhaps more accurately, the need to create meaning is most acute for those of us who struggle with some kind of visible physical anomaly, stigma, chronic illness, or dying, conditions which are constant reminders of one's humanness and finitude. This condition can also be the source for the struggle to prove to others and to oneself that one is worthwhile and capable; that even with the "differentness," one is a legitimate human being with the right to exist.

Acknowledging that illness involves a crisis of meaning, David Barnard sums up Chase Kimball's observation[30] that:

> ...convalescence from illness includes a period of grieving, which he characterizes as mourning the loss of a former self, and building a new self- and world-picture that incorporates the reality of suffering and limitation. ...illness is not merely a biophysical event. It is also a crisis of meaning.

Barnard continues with his own observation:

> ... Illness alters the self-image through changes in bodily form and capability. It disrupts social relationships and the performance of social roles and obligations. It calls exaggerated attention to embodiment and alters the self's ability to manipulate the physical environment according to its own goals. And it prompts questions of the fundamentally benign or hostile character of the cosmos with respect to human striving.[31]

Certain "Why?" questions became very much a part of my life. In the years immediately following the bout with polio (1953–56), I found that one of the best ways to think through my "problems" and thoughts, be they "girl problems," school problems, or whatever, was to walk to the back of the field each day just before sunset and sit on a disk plow which had been left there some years before. From this vantage point, "apart" from the world and in the still silence that often characterizes that time of the day in west Texas, I could let myself get lost in my thoughts. During these "disk plow meditations," I began to feel that there must be some kind of purpose in life; and I began, even then, to consciously search for it:

- What IS the purpose of MY life?
- What is the purpose of ANYONE'S life?
- Just who am I anyway?
- Is there purpose to life?
- What is REALLY important in life?
- What priorities must be established in life?

As these "retreats" continued, an interesting phenomenon began to happen: I was not only aware of having profound feelings, but I was also aware that I was aware! (I now understand that this process of thinking about one's own thinking is called "metacognition.") This led to still further questions:

- Why am *I* struggling over the meaning and purpose of my life?
- Why can't I be like those of my peers who apparently don't have this kind of experience and who don't seem to struggle over such issues?
- Why am I different?

It was also during this same time period that I became fascinated with rocks and fossils; and it would be during some of my rock hunting expeditions on my grandparents' ranch in Concho County that I participated in the "rock experience." As I searched over the ground for rocks, fossils, and arrowheads, my focus of attention would narrow to four- to six-inch square areas. On occasion, I would spot a particular pebble and then consciously begin to put it, and myself, into some kind of perspective. Beginning with the tiny rock and its immediate surroundings, which might amount to only a few square inches and might even include a tiny ant, I would gradually broaden my focus until I had included all that I could see around me. While my spatial perspective expanded to infinity, my time perspective expanded to encompass millions of years. I was placing the tiny rock and myself in relation to each other and in relation to millions of years of geologic history and to millions of light years of space. It was a mind-blowing experience out of which resulted certain "ultimate" questions:

- Who am I?
- Is there a particular reason for my being here on earth, or am I just an accident of history: a "shadow" which appears for a short, futile time, and then is no more?
- How am I related to all of this that I see around me…to that part of existence which I comprehend as I stand here in the middle of this mesquite pasture?
- What does life mean?
- Why am *I* aware of having this experience?

Years later, while I was a staff chaplain in a VA medical center in Kansas, I would have a similar experience with a tiny purple-blue weed flower about the size of a pin head! Occasionally, I would walk across the campus from the psychiatric building to the hospital; and on one of these walks, I looked down and noticed a tiny flower growing on a certain kind of weed. I was fascinated: even this tiny flower, unnoticed by most of the people who walked along here, was a part of God's creation!

Even while I was in the Army, an officer who is supposed to have only practical down-to-earth thoughts, these spiritual experiences continued. Three incidents which occurred while I was stationed at

Fort Benning, Georgia, stand out in particular. On one occasion, during a map reading exercise, I found myself alone in a dry creek bed (we new lieutenants often found ourselves alone in creek beds, some dry and some with water!). As I stopped to "get my bearings," I was suddenly aware of the stillness and silence of that Georgia forest. There was no sound, and the only movement was that of a tiny bird flitting around in a nearby bush. I came away, wondering:

- What just happened?
- Why did it happen to me?
- What does it mean?

The next incident occurred one Sunday morning in the autumn when, instead of going to chapel services, I decided to go for a drive. As I drove along one of the post's back roads, I noticed the morning sun shining through the still-wet autumn leaves. The colors were fabulous shades of red, gold, orange, brown, and yellow. I was immediately impressed by the fact that I was witnessing God's natural version of the stained-glass window! No chapel service could have meant more to me than what I had just experienced. I came away asking *more* questions!

- Why did this happen to *me*?
- Why did I become aware of something as being more than just a phenomenon?
- What does it mean?
- Do others experience things the way I do?
- Do they see things the same way I see them?
- Who am I that I should have such experiences?

The third incident occurred while a friend and I searched through an archeological site on the post. It had been, 150–200 years ago, some kind of residence or home near the bank of a small stream. Now there was nothing left except some bits and pieces of dishes in the dirt and a slowly disappearing clearing where the structure had once stood. As I searched the area, with the sun streaming through the pines, looking for artifacts, I became aware of the quietness and the stillness which pervaded the site. I began to feel that the ground upon which I stood was truly holy…sacred, because human beings had once lived there. I could imagine that they, just like us, had experienced happiness as well as frustration; accomplishments as well as failures; fear and hate as well as love and caring; play and work; birth and death. They, too, had sought meaning and purpose to their existence. And perhaps somewhere…in New York City or Chicago or Houston or Los Angeles, there is someone whose origins can be traced through that site. I walked away from there deep in thought and meditation…inwardly overwhelmed by the thoughts generated.

Once, while visiting family in Texas, several family members went to clean up the cemetery plots of my mother's people in the rural cemetery near Rowena. When we had finished, I drifted around the cemetery reading names and dates etched on stone. At one point, I noticed a couple of small metal markers in one weed-infested corner, walked over, and pulled up some of the weeds. It was the grave of an infant:

- Who was he, this child of the weedy grave?
- Was he or she given a name?
- Where was the mother? How did she feel as she walked away from that tiny grave? Or perhaps she did not even know where he was buried?
- Did ANYONE know this child?
- Where were any relatives? Dallas? Lubbock? Oklahoma City? Did they ever wonder about him?
- What chance did he/she have in life?

– What is life all about that a child, an infant, is buried in the weedy corner of a small country cemetery with only a temporary metal marker to indicate the location…to indicate that, for a short while at least, here was a human being?

I walked away, wondering.

As a staff chaplain in a Veterans Affairs medical center in Leavenworth, Kansas, I conducted over five hundred memorial services in the nearby cemeteries in the twenty-plus years that I was there. Often, before the funeral party arrived, I would go out to the cemetery and walk among the rows and rows of gray-white stones all in military formation. I would read names, dates, places on the various stones, and attempt to understand what life must have been like for those buried there. Each stone represented a human story; the sound of Taps echoing over the gentle hills and the Missouri River bringing an end to each story.

Once, while attending a class in Virginia, I wandered into a nearby National Cemetery and began paging through the directory of the dead buried there. I was awed by the number of "UNKNOWNS" listed there. Most were from the Civil War:

Who were they, these men in Blue and Gray?

Did their parents, their wives, their children know what happened to them?

What does it mean to be human, to be killed in battle and then be buried as an "UNKNOWN"?

These were deeply spiritual experiences for me: they "brought me up short" and forced me to wonder about life, about God, about myself. They drew me into the depths of thought and reflection. These spiritual encounters led me to be aware of something greater than a tiny pebble or stone or the name on a gray-white cemetery marker.

In the early 1970s, as I began my seminary studies, and as I reached a horribly painful period in my need to create a sense of meaning and purpose, I began to type out bits and pieces of thoughts as they flowed forth:

> He felt the will to go on living slowly draining from him; and the thought frightened him. But, as he reflected over this last failure and of the many failures prior to that one, he felt that there HAD to be a reason for all the suffering, anguish, meaninglessness, heartbreak, and loneliness which he had experienced. If there was any reason for him to go on living it was to attempt to find out WHY? to find out the reason for all of the tragedy he had experienced. But, then perhaps he would find in the end that there was no reason; that people would look upon his life as unusually tragic and unfortunate.

> Why did he have to experience so much pain and agony? Yet, he realized that in his suffering, and only in his suffering could he empathize with others who also were suffering. In those few brief moments of happiness and contentment he realized that his thoughts had been superficial. Only when he was plunged into despair and loneliness did his thoughts reach to the bottom of his soul; only then could he see and understand Life; only then could he really FEEL the suffering of others.

> And this too shall pass. It had become a part of his thought processes; a way of looking at life. He began to see everything that happened in its temporal nature. He saw all events in life as fleeting phenomena which were here and then gone. Even life itself was seen as an extremely short event: by the time he was 30 years old he could see, in his mind's eye, the end of the

road of life, he could see death in the distance. Thus, all things became futile. Why struggle for something which will eventually pass?

To him, walking down the road of life was a frustrating task of taking two steps forward and one step back, and not even knowing whether or not one is walking in the right direction.

Sometimes, in the more melancholy moments, it seemed to him that life was the most tragic phenomenon in history. He watched people as they attempted, in one way or another, to create meaning in their lives; as they attempted to find a reason for continuing the struggle for existence. People: they were put here whether or not they really wanted to be here. They had had no choice as to whether or not they were brought into existence. Then they were told, in essence, to survive the best way they could. In order to make the life-struggle "worthwhile," people were given "incentives"—fortune, fame, religion—to keep from destroying themselves. The ultimate "freedom" a person had over his existence was to voluntarily cease to exist. This could take the form of alcohol or drugs, or ultimately, suicide.

When he looked at the whole of life he often wondered if it wasn't just a process people go through to reach death. It seemed like a journey all existing creatures took to reach death. He saw Christianity, and all religion for that matter, as a method of attempting to provide meaning to an otherwise meaningless, involuntary existence. It was an attempt to provide meaning to all of the suffering, heartbreak, loneliness, and anxiety which one inevitably experiences in life.

Suddenly he felt very old and tired—a weariness caused by living. It had been; it continued to be such an exhausting struggle just to find meaning in all of the pain, suffering, and loneliness that he had experienced. Why did all of these things happen to him? There must be some reason!! He realized that if he ever gave up attempting to find the answers it would be the end…

It was inner struggles like this one which exhausted him; made him feel very old. It was inner struggles like this one—those deep, very personal defeats and hurts—which forced him to seek some kind of answers; to seek some kind of meaning to life.

These thoughts (feelings?) were a form of desperate therapy at the time to keep my head "above the water." The most severe crisis points in my life have been those experiences which have dealt with personal meaning, purpose, and self-worth in the face of suffering, loss, pain, and defeat. During those times when meaning, purpose, and self-worth seemed most threatened, I found myself most desperate to find or create new meaning and purposefulness. I could not live in a vacuum. I had to have a reason for being, even if it were the very searching for that reason for being…even if it meant creating personal meaning through the process of searching for meaning! But then, perhaps the search becomes the goal?—to continue the search without "giving up"…without becoming exhausted…without slowing down. All of this becomes the goal!

POLIO

In February 1976, during the time in which I completed the year of Clinical Pastoral Education at the large cancer center, a young girl, nineteen years old, whom I had visited on several occasions, died. As I struggled with my own feelings, I wrote a poem of sorts, struggling to understand how her father, who had spent much time by her bedside as her life ebbed away, must have thought and felt:

A LONG, SAD JOURNEY HOME

> The struggle is finally over.
> "Finally?" It almost sounds sinful:
> It brings on guilt feelings;
> But it is a true response, a true feeling;
> Almost an audible sigh: it is <u>finally</u> over.
>
> She was only 19;
> Eaten up…destroyed…murdered…by Cancer.
> She fought it…we all fought…at first;
> But it was a losing battle, even from the
> beginning, though we didn't realize it.
> God, I feel so helpless…so futile…so damned…
> in the face of that relentless monster,
> Cancer!
>
> The Lord giveth, and the Lord taketh away.
> God damn you Lord!
> Why my little girl…why did You take her away…
> and take her away in such a painful, slow,
> agonizing way?
> If You must execute the young, why don't You
> do it quickly, mercifully?

Those needles and tubes; and tubes and needles.
Bed pans and vomiting that awful blackish-green
liquid from her tortured stomach!
Needles and tubes; probing needles, bloody
arms;
Drip, drip; bottles upon bottles!
Night nurse with flashlight changing bottles;
Am I dreaming? A nightmare!
Pain! Pain! Pain!

A life-size dying doll;
Memories!
Damn them!
They eat through one's numb brain like a
disease!
If I could only forget for only a moment that
she is my flesh and blood;
That I love her;
Things would be so much easier!

They call this life!
I call it hell, not life!
She's there struggling for breath—a dry
rasp coming from deep within.
Perhaps from her very soul?

Why me?
Why her?
Why couldn't it have been me?
Is she in pain?
I'm in pain!
Damn me!

POLIO

Damn my thoughts!

Nurses and doctors and technicians and chaplains
and...
What are they doing here?
What are they doing to my daughter?
Why can't they do something?
They come in and then leave: they are free.
My girl must stay: a prisoner.
I must stay.
God bless them!
God damn them!

God? God? There is no God!
How can a loving God permit such pain and suffering?

I hurt;
I feel numb;
Empty;
Helpless;
Ashamed.
God, I ache!

All these people are suffering;
Dying.
Does anyone out there know the magnitude
of the suffering in here?
They can't;
They don't want to know;
They look the other way.
I hate them.

Grotesque faces;
Missing arms, legs;
Young people looking old;
Old people looking dead;
And here in the midst of all this human
destruction lies my little girl,
Dying.

Dead.
The struggle is finally over.
I'm glad;
I'm sad;
Grieved;
Sickened.

God, it's dark outside;
And cold;
Damp.
Time to go
Time to go home.
Funeral arrangements made.
Good-bye Anderson.
God bless you;
God damn you!

A long, sad journey home.

~ ~ ~ ~ ~ ~ ~ ~ ~ ~ ~

POLIO

Later, as the year at that medical center ended and as I attempted to characterize some of the feelings that the patient must have, I scribbled down these thoughts:

THE PATIENT

The patient; the patient; the patient;
Struggling with cancer;
Hurting with cancer;
Dying of cancer;
The patient; the patient;
The very human patient.

Angry;
Alone;
Afraid;
Afraid to die; afraid of death.
"What lies ahead?" "The 'water' is so
Dark; so murky: O God! What is out
There in front of me? Stand by me, for I
Am so afraid!"

"Don't you people understand? I don't
Want pious words; empty religious cliches!
I just want you to be here with me…
To accept me as I am…to be with me…
Oh, God, I am so alone! Don't desert me
In this terrifying hour…Just be here
With me…Hold my hand…cry with me;
Laugh with me…Let me know that you still
Care."

"Look at all of those people driving by the
Hospital…going to work…going home….
Going shopping…going to a movie. Why
Can't it be one of them instead of me lying
Up here…being eaten up by cancer…fighting
So hard against this monstrous thing within
Me…fighting a losing battle (Oh God let me
Die now! I can't take this pain any longer!)…
Why me? What have I done to deserve this? There
Must be a reason! There is a reason for everything!
And those people out there: Do they realize what
Is going on up here? Do they care? Are they
Afraid to know? Are they running the other way?"

The patient;
Angry;
Alone;
Afraid;
Hurting with cancer;
Dying of cancer;
Hoping;
Hoping against hope;
The patient; the patient;
The very human patient!

~ ~ ~ ~ ~ ~ ~ ~ ~ ~ ~

POLIO

There was a certain hot summer day in the late '70s during which I sat on the warm sand of a dry creek bed in far eastern Colorado with two acquaintances and talked of how Paleo-Indians of the region must have lived and thought. Some days earlier a boy had found an arrowhead near the site, an arrowhead that proved to be many, many years old. It had attracted the attention of people and organizations that are interested in such things and a trained professional "digger" had been sent out to those rolling plains to search for more evidence of early habitation. The digger, an interested farmer, and myself sat in that creek bed in the shade of the cottonwoods, wondering what it must have been like ten thousand…fifteen thousand years ago:

"How did they understand life?"

"What did they believe in?"

"What made them laugh? Cry?"

"Did they, at times, feel that they had failed?"

"What made life meaningful for them?"

"Did they wonder about life?"

In a small rural cemetery just west of Idalia, Colorado, there are four infant graves from one family! FOUR! "Why, God?!?…Why did you take four of my lovely babies??! What have I ever done to you that would deserve such horrible punishment?!?"… In the deafening silence that is in the prairie, she must have walked away, scarred, to attempt to go on with life…to continue to be a mother to any surviving children.

Perhaps because of the polio experience, I have this fierce inner struggle between active involvement with other people and the desire to withdraw "into a place apart": being "in the trenches" versus going to the vast silence of the Big Bend Country of far west Texas where people are only a sometime thing. It is the desire to help others versus "to hell with everybody!" I have a suspicion that much of this struggle is tied to the psycho-spiritual energy that is expended to cope with the paralysis on a daily basis.

There is also the "in-spite-of" versus the "because-of" battle:

Do I go on with life as if nothing had happened?

Can I?

"In spite of" the facial paralysis, I'm going to become an Army officer.

Or am I going to do something in life BECAUSE of the anomaly?

I am going to become a counselor for the handicapped "because" I kinda know what they are going through.

If I follow the latter course, have I "pigeon-holed" myself into a profession that is "good" or appropriate for "cripples?"

As I reflect upon this experience…this personal journey…I realize that one of the greatest motivations or incentives to continue with life was the accepting love and support of my family, relatives, and close friends, especially my fellow students at school in Wall. The fact that my mother was the first-grade teacher there for many years, and that my father was very active in school affairs, probably helped a great deal.

Probably the greatest "ministry" provided by my home church, a congregation of the Unity of the Brethren, was accepting me as a valuable human being, a child of God. I do not remember any of the pastors attempting to deal with any particular theological questions about the polio and the resulting facial paralysis. Perhaps they didn't know or realize that there WERE any theological questions? However, their continuing acceptance, encouragement, and love was the most effective "answer"!

POLIO

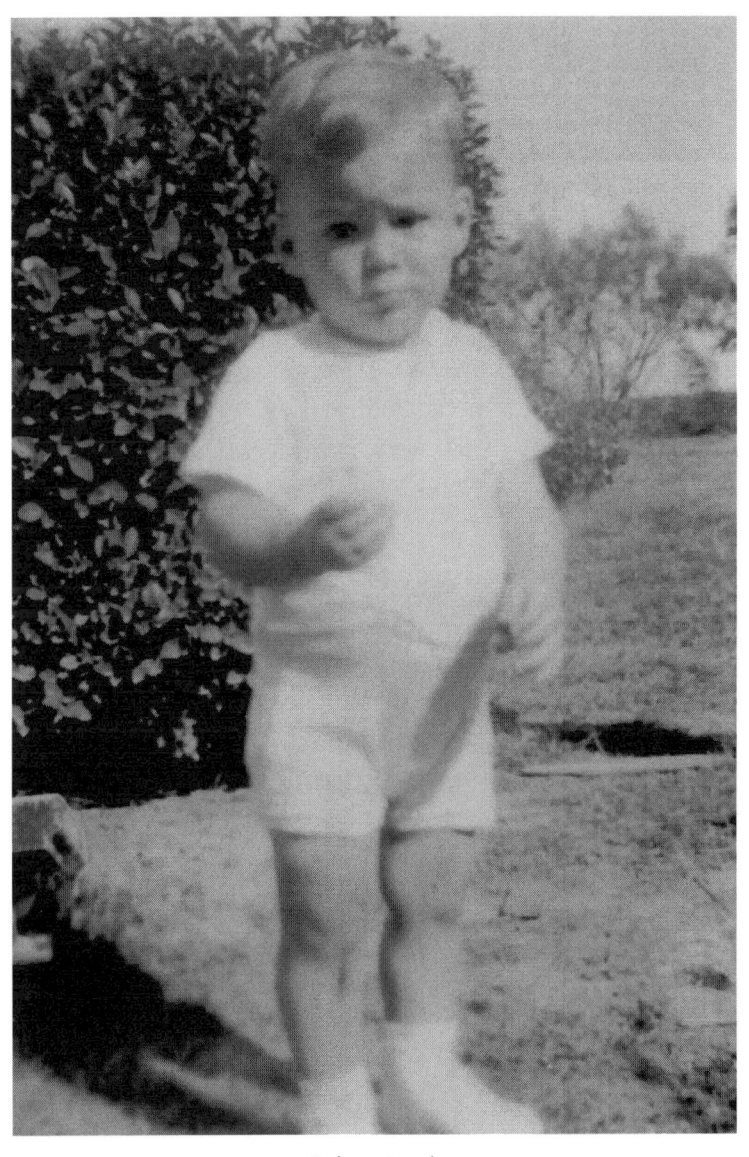

Robert Janek
1942

ROBERT W. JANEK

Eda Lisso Janek (Mom)
Neal and Robert Janek
1942

POLIO

Bill Janek (Dad)
with Robert and older brother, Neal
1942

ROBERT W. JANEK

Neal and Robert Janek
1943

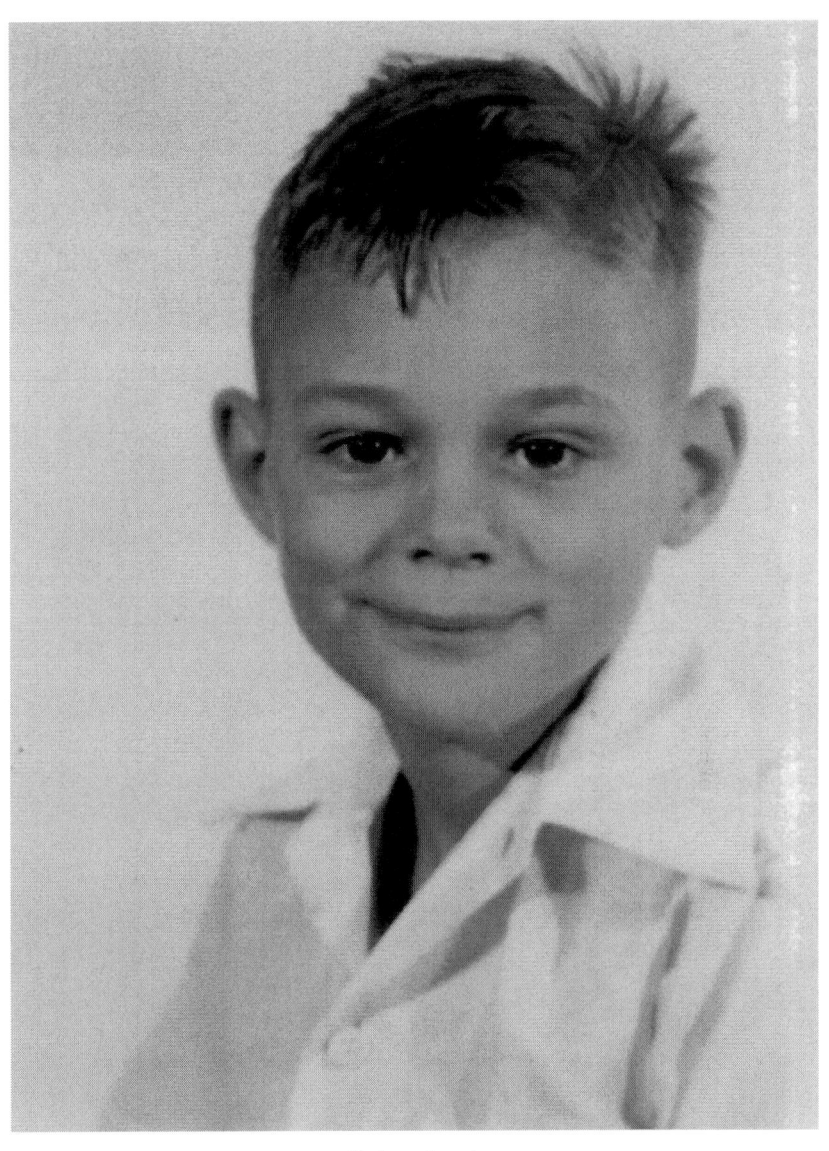

POLIO

Robert Janek
2nd Grade 1947-48

ROBERT W. JANEK

YE TO THE SKY—Robert Janek of Route 2, San Angelo, doesn't need a slide
le to read science-fiction but it helps on other forms of science literature.
nek, like many San Angeloans, has found an increased interest in rockets and
ars.

POLIO

Captain Robert Janek on the canal from Lich Hoi Thuong to Soc Tang, Viet Nam
1966-67

ROBERT W. JANEK

Robert W. Janek
1967
Captain
Armor Branch of the Army
Combat Infantry Badge
After he got back from Vietnam

POLIO

Rev. Robert Janek Kitty = Kenosha
Idalia, Colorado
1977-81

Hospital Chaplain Robert Janek with Santa
Christmas 1999

ROBERT W. JANEK

Chaplain Robert Janek
Dwight D. Eisenhower Dept. of Veteran Affairs Medical Center
Leavenworth, Kanas
2000 ?

POLIO

Robert Janek
November 17, 2019

ROBERT W. JANEK

Jena and Robert Janek

SPIRITUAL REFLECTIONS

I perceive my life as one person's journey of faith, of one unique individual's spiritual pilgrimage, attempting to make this life and the experiences I have had a little more livable, meaningful, and, hopefully, contributive to others. I envision all of us on a spiritual journey or pilgrimage. Each journey is unique: we are exposed to different ideas, and we encounter different opportunities and challenges along that journey; but then perhaps it could be said that every challenge is also an opportunity. In my case, one of the challenges I have encountered is paralytic polio on the left side of my face, a paralysis that is becoming more pronounced as I age.

For the reader, the challenge of my facial paralysis is how the reader will initially, and then eventually, react to my obvious facial paralysis. The opportunity is to grow spiritually from the encounter/relationship with me in this book. For example, will the reader learn to see beyond the paralysis to my essence or inner self; that is, to see that there is more to me than facial paralysis? This same attitude of acceptance applies to all our relationships with other people.

The opportunity/challenge for me has been to work on turning the paralysis into a positive, "contributive" experience: to redeem the pain of life. I have done this within the context of the Christian faith, *as I understand it*, for I realize that different people have very different understandings of the Christian faith and what it means to be a Christian. Christianity, for me, is *not* a destination (unless one considers the journey the destination), but is a journey—an ongoing pilgrimage—that each one of us takes in our own unique pathway. I don't believe that we ever "arrive" at some point of spiritual perfection, some religious goal line, at least in this life. The challenge is to continually grow spiritually throughout life.

As I explored in my previous book, *Thoughts Along the Journey* (1998),[32] perhaps one could say that the heart of my journey is the "Easter Event." It provides hope. First, hope that life is not a meaningless, useless venture or struggle from birth to death...hope that my life has meaning and purpose even if I am unable to clearly discern or understand that meaning. Secondly, there is hope for resurrection...a returning to life...even and especially, in *this* life. God continually gives us the opportunity to start all over again, to have new life, to return to life, to be "born again," not just once but many times! Thirdly, the Easter faith gives me hope that death is not the final victor, that God is Lord over death as well as life.

That Easter event signifies to me that nothing can separate me from the love of God, a God of love whose love is unconditional, a God who *is love*, who will abandon me neither in life nor in death, as reflected in the life, teachings, death, and resurrection of Jesus, who not only gave us a vision of the character of God but who also gave us an idea of how to live life more meaningfully. (More and more, I am seeing that the message of the Gospel—to love one another—is to be applied not just to Christians but to the whole of human civilization: we humans either learn to love one another and the world in which we live, or we will eventually destroy ourselves.) This "Easter Event" allows me a sense of freedom (as well as responsibility) to strive to be all that I can be within the limitations of the human condition as I have experienced it, to strive to seek out and use those talents and abilities that I may possess. It is the freedom to think for myself what it means to be a Christian in the contemporary world with its many uncertainties and ambiguities, that is, the freedom as well as the obligation to doubt, to question, to venture out beyond the realm of normally accepted religious dogmas and doctrine, if necessary, for the sake of personal intellectual and spiritual integrity. This "frightening freedom" allows me to explore all throughout my life my own unique relationship to God, seeking God (and truth) wherever I might find God without necessarily restricting myself to those places where others, or even the church, think I ought to look. I realize that there are those who might brand me as a "agnostic," or as "heterodox" in my beliefs, or an "iconoclast;" but that's okay. My faith in this loving God allows me the freedom to recognize that I do not, and will not, and do not need to have all the answers to life's many complex questions. My faith (trust) in God is often shown more through an attitude toward life and its experiences than an answer. Therefore, I can feel free to continue to expand my horizons and to grow through exploring possible answers to those questions which do arise. I thus see the human as a being who is always potential possibility as well as present reality: the human is always "on the way," always becoming and evolving in many ways, never finished. This in itself is a foundation for hope: with God's help, I have the potential for growth in life, even in the midst of, and perhaps because of, the polio experience. With God's help, I can redeem the polio experience as I travel through life. I can feel free to be open to new ideas, concepts, and interpretations of life, of God, of the nature of the human condition, of the nature and work of Jesus, and of Scripture without feeling threatened by these new ideas and understandings, realizing that all such ideas, concepts, doctrines, and even biblical interpretations are "man-made." This awareness in turn leads to a certain "humility" and tentativeness in my own theology, allowing me to be open to new, more meaningful, relevant possibilities in understanding God, life, and the world around me. I am not much into "absolutes," except perhaps for the idea of the love of God, and even my understanding of that changes or evolves over the years as I experience life. My trust in this loving, forgiving, compassionate God, who knows something about the limitations and potential of the being God has created, gives me the freedom to recognize that I am far from perfect; that I am a very human person who possesses weaknesses as well as strengths, a person who experiences failures as well as successes, hope as well as anxieties and fears. This trust allows me to admit my own emotions and feelings, be they of anger or of joy, of sadness or of fear or jealousy.

Theologically, therefore, I interpret my polio experience as one of those experiences that a person is susceptible to in life because one is a human being. In one sense, I would call it an "accident of history" or an "accident of historical circumstance," that is, I happened to be a young person (eleven years old) growing up in a time when polio was a widespread reality; and due to certain biological/physical factors, I happened to contract it…a "coincidence," if you will. Life happens. I firmly believe that Christians, no matter how devout, are as "vulnerable" to life as is the most "devout atheist" (as a cancer patient once described herself). It is what we Christians do with what happens to us that ultimately counts. I think that this is important to remember, for, from this perspective or personal interpretation, the theological "Why did God do this to me?" question that many people ask during times of suffering and crisis begins to take on less urgency. This understanding of my polio experience also, of course, says something about my image or understanding or definition of God: I do not see God as a being who is in absolute, total control of every small detail of my life.

I do not believe, for example, that my having polio was a part of some overall, eternal, premeditated, predetermined, predestined "Divine plan" for my life. That is, I don't believe that somewhere in the distant past, God decided to create a person who would be named Robert who would, at the age of eleven, contract polio in the late summer of 1952. I cannot remember *anytime* that I did believe this. To me, such an understanding of God and how God works within the world strips us of any freedom to choose: we become only puppets manipulated by God...some kind of wind-up toy that goes through certain predetermined motions. I even struggle over the concept of choice. I think that our freedom of choice goes just so far, and that our choices are affected or influenced by previous choices and their results; by our basic inherited biological makeup; and by environmental influences such as family, peers, social conditions, education, religious background, etc. I think that we bring a lot of "baggage" (past experiences, biases, etc.) to each decision we make, which in turn becomes a part of the baggage we take to the next decision! This applies not only to our decision-making process, but also to what we believe about (and how we perceive) God, ourselves, and the world around us.

Further, related to the above, I do not believe that God has a deliberate, preconceived plan for my life. God may HOPE that my life will follow a certain set of guidelines (e.g., that I will be a loving, caring, forgiving, sensitive, understanding person in whatever I do); however, I don't believe that God has mapped out every detail in my life. For example, I do not believe that God knows what is going to happen to me, or what kinds of decisions I will make, next Friday at 3:32 P.M.

Neither do I believe that God "gave" me polio for some specific, deliberate reason, such as, for example, punishment. I cannot believe that God, at least the caring, loving, compassionate, understanding, forgiving, self-sacrificing God I believe in, would "punish" a barely eleven-year-old child so severely for some "crime" or some "sin" that child supposedly committed.

Neither do I believe that God was, for some reason, punishing my parents (or anyone else) by striking ME down with paralyzing polio. To me, such a concept of "justice" is sick! All too often, this understanding is used to excuse and defend God, as if God needs defending!

However, I am aware that many of us can dredge up enough guilt feelings from perceived "sins" of the past that we can easily interpret any pain or failure or suffering or misfortune as "Divine punishment!" Indeed, some of us may even welcome some kind of punishment from God for some horrendous sin we feel we have committed, if for no other reason than to get on with life without the burden of that "sin" continuing to weigh us down!

Of course, our way of life or lifestyle and our attitudes can bring on a lot of "bad" experiences, illness, accidents, etc.; however, I do not interpret these as deliberate punishments from God. If we do "dumb" things (such as driving ninety miles an hour down a winding dirt road just for the fun of it), if we make bad decisions, "bad" things can result, God or no God! I refuse to blame God for my being overweight, for some of the really bad decisions I have made, or even for my having contracted polio.

If we believe that our misfortunes (illness, accidents, disabilities, etc.) are "Divine punishment," then the person experiencing the misfortune is going to feel guilty, at times for things she/he should not feel guilty about. The "guilty" person is going to feel like a "great sinner," perhaps even unworthy of God's love and forgiveness. Such a person will consequently be vulnerable to others who feel a sense of moral superiority and spiritual self-righteousness toward that person; others who feel that he/she is "fair game" for moral preaching and exhortation; others who will use that person's sense of guilt and shame to manipulate him/her into doing things which satisfy the manipulator, for example, contribute to some religious cause or organization, to join a particular church, and/or "witness" to others of his/her "sin" and of God's "loving" punishment and forgiveness. (A parish minister once told me that in order to get the people of one's congregation to support various of his church projects, he was required to make them feel guilty!)

And the idea that God was punishing me—an eleven-year-old—to get me to love God, or love God more than I supposedly did, is ridiculous! Do we humans believe that we can get others to love us more if we just punish them?

Further, I don't believe that God was deliberately "educating" me or attempting to "teach me a lesson," or "preparing me for some great religious mission or a life of religious work," or "testing" me to see if I had "enough faith." What kind of parents would deliberately devastate her or his child's physical health and wound him or her psychologically in order to educate him or prepare her for some mission, or to test him or even punish him? Such a parent would be considered psychologically unstable, even sent to prison! How then could I attribute such actions to God? Kyle Johnson has a term for this: "Theopathology," that is, "...ascribing a personality or behavior trait to God which would be considered psychopathological in a human."[33]

Tragically, many Christians, in order to "defend God," do just this! I don't believe that God needs defending; and I would suggest that the felt need to defend God is the product of bad theology.

Several authors have addressed this issue:

Philip Hansen has written:

> What more terrible tribute to God is there than to attempt to win people for Him by threatening those who don't want Him that they will go to hell? That's like a young man asking his girl to marry him and, if she doesn't", threatening to kill her.[34]

Michael Cavanagh has observed:

> To the extent that we fear God, we can't authentically love God. What may look and feel like love is actually identification with the aggressor. Analogously, a youth may join a tough gang, not because he loves the gang, but because the gang is less likely to hurt one of its own members. People who fear God's wrath have fear, not

love, in their hearts. They want to get close to and placate God, so God won't hurt them.[35]

And, Charles Hartshorne has said:

> ... The traditional idea... is that good behavior in this life must be motivated by concern for one's welfare after death. People, it was thought, are not to be trusted to love their neighbors in this life unless they have something for themselves to hope for or fear after they die. We are to gamble with God about rewards and punishments in a later life earned by how we respond to divine commands in this life.
> ...
> Is it really necessary, in order to induce good behavior in people, to convince them that they will be rewarded or punished after death for the way they have lived?
>
> ...the unfreedom of behavior controlled by threats and promises, the reliance on naked self-interest is repellent once one sees it for what it is, a confession of disbelief in love as the principle of principles, and a glorification of egocentricity. ...
>
> Unless being loving is its own reward it is not really loving.[36]

It has been my experience, from my own life, and from working with many others in a pastoral care role, that suffering is *extremely neutral*, that is, experiencing pain and disappointment and defeat does not automatically make us a better or more religious or more pious person… does not automatically draw us closer to God! In this, I especially appreciate the observations of such people as Harold Kushner who wrote:

> Does God "temper the wind to the shorn lamb"? Does he never ask more of us than we can endure? My experience, alas, has been otherwise. I have seen people crack under the strain of unbearable tragedy. I have

seen marriages break up after the death of a child...I have seen some people made noble and sensitive through suffering, but I have seen many more people grow cynical and bitter...If God is testing us, He must know by now that many of us fail the test. If He is only giving us burdens we can bear, I have seen Him miscalculate far too often.[37]

As Paul Tournier expressed:

> ... Things and events, whether fortunate or unfortunate, are simply what they are, morally neutral. What matters is the way we react to them. Only rarely are we the masters of events, but (along with those who help us) we are responsible for our reactions.
> ...
> For the few hundreds of orphans listed by Rentchnick who have made a name for themselves in history, there are millions whom deprivation in childhood has handicapped for life.[38]

As Leonard Bowman who wrote:

> Despite the success stories, hero stories, and examples of what is possible for the handicapped person, the more common story is one of struggle, repeated frustration, and shattered self-respect.[39]

As John Hick reflected:

> ...although there are many striking instances of good being triumphantly brought out of evil through a person's reaction to it, there are many other cases in which the opposite has happened. Sometimes obstacles breed strength of character, dangers evoke courage and unselfishness, and calamities produce patience and moral steadfastness. On the other hand, sometimes they lead to resentment, fear, grasping selfishness, and disintegration of character.[40]

As Charles Meyer affirmed but then added:

> Of course it is sometimes true that suffering can be an occasion for redemption, for the healing of memories, relationships, hurts, fears, or guilts. Pain and illness often are the precipitators of change in behavior or perspective on the person's lifestyle. But suffering is also quite often the occasion for unquenchable bitterness, debilitating despair, collapse of faith and disintegration of personhood.

> …in our attempts to make sense of an illness we want to believe there is some purpose, some plan, some reason for the horrible suffering we or our loved ones are enduring. … Once again, the truth is that suffering is as amoral as the virus, bacteria, or systemic condition that is its cause.[41]

As George Gurley wrote in the *Kansas City Star*:

> …There's nothing intrinsically enriching about suffering except insofar as one looks into one's soul and tries to learn something from it.

> …There is nothing dignified about suffering. Suffering is mean and hard and difficult and very often it hardens people and demeans them.

> On the other hand, to transcend suffering, to see in it a learning experience, then it has value. … Was there any value in my mother's death when I was 11? Well, it was a great tragedy and it twisted my life. But I was able to extricate some value out of it much later in life. Would I trade my mother's life for that? You bet I would not. If we have to choose between the value we get out of suffering and not having the suffering, I'd rather not have the suffering.[42]

And as Bart Ehrman concludes:

> ... Sometimes something good can come out of suffering.
>
> At the same time, I am absolutely opposed to the idea that we can universalize this observation by saying that something good *always* comes out of suffering. The reality is that *most* suffering is not positive, does not have a silver lining, is not good for the body or soul, and leads to wretched and miserable, not positive, outcomes.
>
> ... A lot of times, what does not kill you completely incapacitates you, mars you for life, ruins your mental or physical well-being – permanently. We should never, in my view, take a glib view of suffering – our own or that of others.
>
> I especially, and most vehemently, reject the idea that someone else's suffering is designed to help *us*. ... Sure, our *own* suffering may, on occasion, make us better people, stronger, or more considerate and caring, or more humane. But other people do not – decidedly do not – suffer in order to make us happier or nobler.[43]

There seem to be at least three general responses to or results of physical or emotional/psychological suffering. FIRST, people can be crushed by it, especially if they experience too much of it, or too much of it in a relatively short space of time; and/or if they do not receive adequate loving emotional support along with it. I have known people who became very bitter and vengeful because of painful life experiences. Others drown their psychological and/or physical pain in drugs and alcohol. Still, others withdraw into themselves in order to avoid further pain and suffering, especially when they have been hurt by human relationships. Others, who believe that suffering is punishment from

God, can lose their faith, angry that God punished them far more than any "crime" that they may have committed warranted. Many people, especially "church-going" people, grow up with the notion (erroneous, I believe) that if you are a "good, faithful, believing Christian" and you attend church regularly nothing "bad" is going to happen to you. Thus, one believes that life should be a bowl of cherries: "God is good!" As one's life journey progresses, and "bad" things begin to happen, as they inevitably will, a person begins to feel (1) betrayed by this supposedly "good" God who should have protected him/her; (2) guilty for not having strong enough faith; and/or (3) cynical toward the whole idea of the existence of a loving God.

SECOND, people can grow from suffering, becoming more aware of and sensitive to others' pain; and thus wanting, in some way, to help alleviate as much suffering as is humanly possible. For example, while I do not believe that God was consciously and deliberately attempting to teach me something or to make me a "better" person or to strengthen my personal faith by "giving" me polio (if I had been taught in church that God is the great cosmic protector, I could have just as easily walked away from Christianity: God didn't protect me!), I do hope that I did learn a few things from the experience!

I hope that I learned that even innocent people (even the most devout Christian) experience suffering, not just those people who have committed some horrible sin; that God does not "protect" God's favorites from the human condition. Once, while visiting patients in a VA medical center during one of those wild and crazy Kansas thunderstorms during which there was a tornado alert, a patient assured me that I, a chaplain, had nothing to worry about! God would protect me! I assured him that God would no more "protect" me than anyone else in that hospital! Having all the faith in the world does not protect us from the pain of being human, as if believing hard enough will provide some kind of Divine insulation or shield from the human condition! I believe that being a Christian doesn't so much protect us from the human condition as it helps us creatively, redemptively, and contributively cope with the pain of it!

Further, I hope that I have learned through my polio experience that there are more important values, goals, and priorities in life than the accumulation of material things, or even the accumulation of knowledge…that loving, caring relationships are ultimately more important than how far up the "ladder of success" I can climb…that service to others is ultimately more satisfying.

I hope, also, that I have learned that one must attempt to look beyond a person's physical, outward appearance to her/his inner spiritual character. To a great extent, a person cannot help the way she/he looks, but that a person DOES have some control over the way he/she lives life…over the kinds of values and priorities and goals by which he/she lives life.

I hope that I have learned to be, or perhaps more accurately, to STRUGGLE to be, more aware of and sensitive to the suffering of others: a kind of "existential empathy" (well, it sounds good) with others. Only as I am willing and able to recognize and accept the pain that I experience am I able to appreciate and minister to the pain that others experience.

When I think of what this "redemptive existential empathy" is like, I am reminded of the elderly veteran patient I once visited in the VA. As he told his life story, which was over eighty years long, he said: "Chaplain, there have been times when I have stood at the abyss and looked over. I backed away from taking that last step; but I can appreciate those who did take that step over the abyss." He did not condemn them. He did not say that they had sinned by committing suicide. He did not refer to them as cowards. He had "been there," he could empathize, he could understand, he could appreciate the decision that they had made.

Finally, I hope that I have learned that God's love and presence are expressed through the love and care of very human people, even through me!

Perhaps it would be more accurate to say that I hope I *am learning* these kinds of things from my polio experience in that learning is a lifelong process. Further, I suspect that if we can get away from the belief that our suffering is some kind of divine punishment or testing, then we will be more open to learning and growing from it. We will not feel a need to hide it or depreciate it out of a sense of guilt or shame, and instead, will struggle to make the suffering more meaningful. We will see God helping us redeem the pain of life rather than being the cause of it.

Further, while I don't believe that God "gave" me polio to strengthen my faith, I do hope that my faith was strengthened in that I have developed a more mature, a more realistic understanding of God and how God works in the world than I would have otherwise.

Unfortunately, there is a THIRD response to personal suffering. I suspect that in many cases of suffering, people neither grow from it nor are diminished by it. They just "sweep it under the rug"—often tragically, in the name of religious faith or belief, which says that if you have enough faith, you will not suffer or experience pain or defeat or physical disability, etc.—and go on with life as if nothing had happened. And perhaps this is the most tragic response of all: personal suffering has become a wasted experience.

Related to this, I would suggest that there are at least two kinds of "healing": physical healing and spiritual healing. For some of us, physical healing, at least at this point in medical/technological advances, is not possible; however, spiritual healing can still take place whether or not there is physical healing. Spiritual healing in relation to physical disabilities/anomalies takes place when we accept our situation and turn it into a contributive experience. We "redeem the pain of life"; we grow in appreciation, understanding, empathy, patience, caring, forgiveness, and openness toward others. On the other hand, physical healing can take place without spiritual healing: we learn nothing from the experience; we do not grow spiritually from the experience; we go on with life as if nothing had happened. We can be physically healed without becoming more empathetic or understanding, without becoming more sensitive, without becoming more compassionate, without becoming more grateful.

As I said before, I personally do not have to believe that there is some kind of consciously planned deliberate divine purpose for everything that happens to me. I don't have to believe that each and every thing that happens to me has some kind of divine or cosmic meaning or ultimate purpose behind it. I think that it is up to us to create meaning from it. I believe that there are many things that happen to us that are no one's "fault" or part of some deliberate divine plan. They just happen. The task of the Christian, as I see it, is to make something positive, redemptive, creative, meaningful, and "contributive" out of the experience: to "redeem the pain"; as they say, "to make lemonade out of the lemons of life." In my case, surely God was with me in that sick bed as much as God was with the healthy child in her bed and with the child who died from polio.

However, I encounter many people who find that they can cope better with "bad" experiences if and when they believe that there is some divine reason for the experiences, even if they cannot discern that reason.

Let me now comment upon my use of the word "contributive" that I have used when referring to possible results of or responses to suffering and "bad" experiences. I think that one of the greatest possible results of or responses to the painful experiences we encounter in the course of life is to learn something from them by which we can then *contribute* to the well-being of others…by which we can make others' lives a little more livable. A central part of this process is what I call "redemptive existential empathy": through reflection of our own personal experiences, and observation of others' experiences, then developing an appreciation for what it means to be human, an appreciation then translated into a compassionate, understanding, caring contributive lifestyle. For example, perhaps we can lift up to others, in our daily actions as well as in our words, a different set of values…a different measure of success…by which to live; by which to judge the quality of one's life. Perhaps one can show others a new appreciation of beauty; or the awareness that others also hurt; or to show that the truly eternal values in life are personal qualities such as honesty, fairness, personal integrity, patience, caring, forgiveness, service to others, an openness to learn, loving, the struggle to understand and appreciate others…

One approach to turning sour or "bad" experiences into contributive experiences is to pause and reflect upon what happened, and then to ask oneself three basic questions, whose answers are then lived out in one's life:

(1) "What or who helped me through this bad experience; and why or how did it help?"
(2) "What or who did NOT help me through this experience; and what was it about this that did NOT help?"
(3) "What could have or would have helped me through this that did not happen?"

Let me give an example from my own life. What helped me when my father died in 1961 was the awkward outpouring of concern and care by the many people of that farming community. Many came to our front door with food, and with fumbling but well-meant words of consolation and sorrow. What did NOT help were the extremely conservative theological (anti-Roman Catholic) words of one of the ministers performing the memorial service. I felt ashamed and embarrassed because I knew that many of the people in attendance, long-time friends and neighbors of my father's, were Roman Catholic.

Here's another example of this three-step reflective process. What helps me when I am hurting is someone who will listen…someone who will appreciate my pain, my anxiety, my fear, my sense of loneliness… someone who will attempt to empathize with my situation, drawing from that person's own personal experiences of woundedness. What does NOT help is for the person to ridicule my feelings:

- "Oh, you're just a wimp!"
- "Grown men don't cry."
- "Oh, you shouldn't feel that way!"
- "If you think you have it bad, look at that person over there!"

Or, as one extremely insensitive dentist once remarked:

- "Oh, I have had ten-year-olds who could handle more pain than you!"

Needless to say, I never went back to THAT dentist!

Or a person who will change the subject to something less threatening to that person; or who will play a game of "suffering-one-upmanship":

"If you think you have it bad, let me tell you MY story!"

The first two steps are easiest: What helped (feel gratitude)? … What did NOT help (feel anger, bitterness, grudges, revenge, etc.)? It may be tempting to stop here, wanting to distance oneself from the pain as soon and as far as possible.

The third step calls one deeper into reflective thought:

- What could have or would have helped me through this experience that did not happen?"

During this period of crisis, what would have helped to get through it? Perhaps the loving presence of a "significant other," or a soft human touch, or someone who did not feel the need to provide "pat answers" to one's dilemma, or someone who had been through a similar experience who could empathize, or someone who continued to love the person even though the person felt unlovable, or someone who had been willing to listen and could comfortably handle the silences.

Then comes the commitment and resolve to use this painful experience and these reflective thoughts to become a means of healing, empathetic love toward others who are caught up in difficult circumstances ("redemptive existential empathy"). This outreach to others is not so much to share one's own story of pain (although occasionally a few words could prove helpful), as it is to give full attention at the moment to trying to feel what it must be like to be in this other person's shoes, listening, probing, listening, asking questions, listening, holding a hand, listening, *listening*! It is such a rare experience for a person to be deeply heard by someone who seems truly interested that when it does happen, it is a vehicle of release and healing. When a person brings an empathetic ear because he/she, too, knows what it is to be wounded, that person is an agent in the healing process! And therein lies meaning and purpose—using the past painful bad experiences of life not to dwell upon the regurgitating bitterness, but to turn and reach out to help others out of the depths of their physical/emotional/spiritual pain.

Earlier, I mentioned the word "reflect." I did so because I believe that it is an extremely valuable and important process in making lemonade out of the lemons of life. Without reflecting upon our personal experiences and struggling with the three questions I listed, the experiences will become wasted experiences.

Unfortunately, in America at least, the process of taking time for reflection is frowned upon. Anyone caught quietly reflecting or meditating (except cloistered Roman Catholic monks and Quakers) is considered wasting his/her time and/or of being lazy. How many of us have felt self-conscious, even embarrassed, when we were sitting on the front porch in a time of quiet contemplation, watching the hummingbirds feed, and some acquaintance drove by and saw us? Eugene Bianchi, spoke of this when he observed:

> ...the preponderant conditioning of technological culture opposes the inward journey as a threat to the ethos of man-the-producer. The contemplative life is thought to be opposed to the full-time energy required for productive purposes.[44]

We Protestants, especially, feel very uncomfortable with silence and silent meditation, particularly in our worship services! Once, years ago, my wife and I attended a "silent Quaker" service in Denver during which the people came in, sat down, and remained in silent meditation and reflection for forty-five minutes! I timed it! Then out of this silent reflective, listening time, gradually, individuals began to speak their truth, the insights they received in the silence. Try that in a Protestant church sometime!

Yet, until we are willing to get in touch with our own feelings and thoughts, we cannot appreciate or understand the feelings and thoughts of others; and thus, cannot really effectively and compassionately minister to them in their time of need.

I don't believe that God consciously, deliberately does things to a particular person for some particular reason that God has in mind. I believe that as we humans journey through life, we are susceptible to or subject to or vulnerable to a variety of "bad" experiences. The important thing is *how* we react to them, that is, it is not necessarily what happens to us, but how we react to the things that happen to us that counts. It is the process of moving from the *theological Why?* question (for which there is most often no adequate answer) to the *Now-that-it-has-happened-what-am-I-going-to-do-about-it?* kind of question.

I emphasize the *theological Why?* because I find that there are various levels of *Why?* questions when one is struggling with something that happened. The *Why?* may refer to the medical or physical reason that an illness occurred (high cholesterol, high blood sugar, an inherited gene). The *Why?* may refer to the physical reason a particular accident occurred ("The brakes failed"), or it may refer to the politico-economic reason for the outbreak of a war, or to the psychological reasons for the break-up of a relationship. These kinds of *Why?* questions are normally fairly easily, if not without great complexity, answered. It's the *theological Why?* that causes the most inner struggle and pain, especially if one believes that everything that happens, happens at the deliberate instigation of God.

Thus, I see the *role* of God not so much as one of protecting the *faithful* from the various pains of being human, as it is to help us through the bad times…*to help us make lemonade out of the lemons of life*… to help us turn otherwise seemingly meaningless, devastating, worthless, and wasted experiences into meaningful, purposeful, *contributive* experiences. In other words, God is there to help us redeem the pain…to create meaning. As Harvey Potthoff said:

> God is present in adversity as that reality in the light of which experiences which have been counted wasted, evil, or tragic may be gathered into some new pattern of meaning, purpose, and wholeness. The reality of God is mediated by persons who reveal that adversity can be redemptive.[45]

To me, to be in a loving relationship with God does *not* mean that God is going to protect me from the negative side of the human condition, but instead that God's loving me means that I am important enough to struggle to overcome the adverse aspects of the human condition, i.e., that I am worth the effort. In my case, to believe that God loves me means that I am just as important to God as anyone else and thus gives me the energy and encouragement to creatively live with the paralysis.

Therefore, in my polio experience, I understand God's love at work *not* in having deliberately caused it for some particular reason (Of course, I suppose that one could argue that God created a world in which polio is a reality!), but in helping me make something meaningful and contributive out of it. I see God's love helping me to struggle to learn to accept the facial paralysis as being a part of who I am, without the feelings of shame or guilt or inferiority, and accepting that fact creatively and contributively. It is a challenge to be creatively overcome rather than a burden to be shamefully borne.

I see the love of God at work in those many people who stood by me and encouraged me *to be all that I could be* and accepted me as I was, and am, as God accepts me…those persons who were, and are, able to look beyond the facial paralysis to see and appreciate a real, legitimate human being with talents and abilities and personal worth and potential as well as a few hang-ups, flaws, and quirks!…those people who felt and feel that I should have the same opportunities to succeed and fail as anyone else…those people who continue to love me and care about me. I understand God's love to be at work among those caring, accepting people who related and relate to me without preconceived notions that suffering is a deliberate punitive action by God, and therefore, that I should be treated accordingly. Out of this personal understanding of God's love in my life, I believe that it is my task to "go and do likewise."

I think that we can argue forever over theological reasons for suffering; however, I very much doubt that we will ever reach a solution that fits *all* situations of suffering in human life, that is, an answer that pleases or satisfies everyone. In this, I appreciate what Daniel Simundson had to say:

> … Since all of our answers to the 'why' of human suffering are only partial, contextual, penultimate, they can never explain every example of human suffering. Though each answer can have value for a certain person and time and place, each may also bring problems because the mysteries of suffering cannot be contained in a single intellectual proposition.
>
> …

The danger is to be so satisfied with our own system for explaining human suffering that we begin to apply it in more general and universal ways. ... What I have devised as beneficial for me may not be right for you, and I must resist the temptation to force you to accept my favorite explanations of suffering.[46]

Alexander Feinsilver observes of the Jewish tradition:

... Men of every creed and culture have raised the question, Why is there pain and evil in this world, and why do the righteous sometimes suffer? Our (Jewish) tradition is wise enough not to be dogmatic about the answer, wise enough to recognize that all answers have somehow been inadequate.
...
... Tragedy and disease should not be attributed to an "act of God." They may be due to human cupidity and human stupidity. Many diseases that once beset mankind have been brought under control, and some have been completely eliminated. ... What is so often called an "act of God" may well be the result of our failure to use the gifts of mind and heart we possess for the benefit of mankind. To call sorrow and suffering an "act of God" can be a case of "passing the buck" instead of facing up to our own responsibilities.
...
If we cannot fully explain sorrow and suffering, we ought perhaps to ask, How can we use them? How can we use them creatively?
...
Man, from the standpoint of Judaism, is akin to God; he is challenged to assert the capacities within him, to use his gifts of mind and heart to reduce or remove the sorrow and suffering that beset the human family.[47]

Thus, it seems to me that the ultimate "answer" to the problem of human suffering is people working with people to overcome unnecessary suffering where possible and to make "necessary" suffering more tolerable...even redemptive. That is, in a very real sense, how the *theological Why?* question of suffering is answered, not through intellectual speculation or theological platitudes, but through the very human *love in action*. I feel that the presence of God is in the loving act. We become, through the awareness of our own pain, aware of the pain and suffering of humanity (*redemptive existential empathy*). We then begin to deal with it on a day-to-day basis, alleviating the causes of suffering, if possible, and making inevitable suffering less painful, less destructive of the spirit, and more redemptive.

Since I am not God possessing all the answers, all knowledge, I tend to be tentative in my thinking, trying to be open to new ways of seeing and understanding God, how God works in the world, and what it means to be Christian.

I am one of those Christians who believe God is much more interested in my struggling to love others than in my having a proper *theology*...than in any *right beliefs* I should have.

The journey continues....

Notes

Preface

1. Loren Eiseley, *The Immense Journey* (New York: Vintage Books, 1957), p. 13.

Definitions Used and Questioned

2. Beatrice Wright, *Physical Disability – A Psychosocial Approach*, *Second Edition* (New York: Harper & Row, 1983), p.11.
3. Erving Goffman, *Stigma – Notes on the Management of Spoiled Identity* (Englewood Cliffs, New Jersey: Prentice-Hall, 1963), p. 5.
4. Beatrice Wright, *Physical Disability – A Psychosocial Approach*, *Second Edition*, p. 17.
5. Loren Eiseley, *The Immense Journey*, p. 13.

Introduction

The Beginning

6. Eda Sarah Lisso Janek, Robert's mother, written in the late 1980s in San Angelo, Texas.
7. Eda Janek recalled more in her own autobiographical notes.

The Journey

8. Hugh Gregory Gallagher, *FDR's Splendid Deception* (New York: Dodd, Mead, & Company, 1985), p xi.
9. *Holy Bible – New Revised Standard Version*, Leviticus 21:18–20.
10. Erving Goffman, *Stigma: Notes on the Management of Spoiled Identity*, pp. 14–15.
11. Erving Goffman, *Stigma: Notes on the Management of Spoiled Identity*, p. 14.
12. Harvey Potthoff, *God and the Celebration of Life* (Chicago: McNally & Company, 1969), p 28.
13. Beatrice Wright, *Physical Disability – A Psychosocial Approach, Second Edition*, p. 19.
14. Beatrice Wright, *Physical Disability – A Psychosocial Approach, Second Edition*, pp. 332, 334.
15. *Twenty-Four Hours a Day – Reading for November 12. (Center City, Minnesota:* Hazelden Press, 1975).
16. Leonard Bowman, *The Importance of Being Sick – A Christian Reflection* (USA: A Consortium Book, 1976), pp. 175–176.
17. Hugh Gregory Gallagher, *FDR's Splendid Deception*, pp. 29–30.
18. Beatrice Wright, *Physical Disability – A Psychosocial Approach, Second Edition*, p. 64.
19. H. Zur Meng, Sozialpsychologie der Körperbeschädigten: Ein Beitrag zum Problem der praktischen Psychohygiene. *Schweizer*

Archiv für Neurologie und Psychiatrie, 1938, *40*, 328–344. (Reported in Barker et al., 1953.)

20. R. G. Barker, B. A. Wright, L. Myerson, & M. R. Gonick, *Adjustment to physical handicap and illness: A survey of the social psychology of physique and disability* (2nd ed.). New York: Soc. Sci. Res. Council, Bull. 55, 1953.

21. F. C. Macgregor, T. M. Abel, A. Bryt, E. Lauer, & S. Weissmann, *Facial deformities and plastic surgery* (Springfield, Ill.: Charles C Thomas, 1953), pp. 70–71, 77, 79.

22. Erving Goffman, *Stigma: Notes on the Management of Spoiled Identity*, p. 5.

23. Erik Erickson, *Dimensions of a New Identity* (New York: Norton Publishers, 1974), p. 96.

24. Erving Goffman, *Stigma: Notes on the Management of Spoiled Identity*, p. 10.

25. W. Y. Baker and L. H. Smith, "Facial Disfigurement and Personality," *Journal of the American Medical Association*, CXII (1939), p. 303.

26. Hugh Gregory Gallagher, *FDR's Splendid Deception*, pp. xi–xii.

27. Eugene Kennedy, *If You Really Knew Me Would You Still Like Me? – Building Self Confidence* (Allen, Texas: Thomas More, A Division of RCL – Resources for Christian Living, 1975), pp. 6, 9, 10, 12.

28. Leonard Bowman, *The Importance of Being Sick – A Christian Reflection*, pp. 212.

29. Robert M. Baird. "Meaning in Life: Discovered or Created?" *Journal of Religion and Health*, Volume 24(2) (Summer 1985), pp. 118, 123.

30. Chase Kimball, *The Biopsychosocial Approach to the Patient* (Baltimore: Williams and Wilkins, 1981).

31. David Barnard, "Illness as a Crisis of Meaning: Psycho-

Spiritual Agendas in Health Care," *Pastoral Psychology*, Volume 33(2) (Winter 1984), pp. 74–82.

Spiritual Reflections

32. Robert W. Janek, *Thoughts Along the Journey* (Leavenworth, Kansas: Forest of Peace Publishing, Inc., 1998), pp. 33-35.
33. Kyle D. Johnson. "Theopathology: Concept Assessment, Intervention," *The Journal of Pastoral Care*, Volume XLV(3) (Fall 1991), p. 245.
34. Philip Hanson, *Sick and Tired of Being Sick and Tired* (Minneapolis: Park Printing, 1989) p. 75.
35. Michael Cavanagh. "The Perception of God in Pastoral Counseling." *Pastoral Psychology*, Volume 41(2) (1992), p. 76.
36. Charles Hartshorne, *Omnipotence and Other Theological Mistakes* (State University of New York, 1984) pp. 97–99.
37. Harold Kushner, *When Bad Things Happen to Good People* (New York: Schocken Books, 1981), p. 26.
38. Paul Tournier, *Creative Suffering* (San Francisco: Harper & Row, 1981), pp. 29, 31.
39. Leonard Bowman, *The Importance of Being Sick – A Christian Reflection*, pp. 175–176.
40. John Hick, *Philosophy of Religion – Fourth Edition* (New Jersey: Prentice Hall, 1990), p. 47.
41. Charles Meyer, *Surviving Death: A Practical Guide to Caring for the Dying and Bereaved* (Mystic, Connecticut: Twenty-Third Publications, 1988), pp. 32–33.
42. George Gurley, an article written in *The Kansas City Star* (Thursday, March 2, 1995, p. F–6.
43. Bart D. Ehrman, *God's Problem: How the Bible Fails to Answer Our Most Important Question: Why We Suffer*, pp. 155–156.

44. Eugene C. Bianchi, *Aging as Spiritual Journey* (New York: Crossroad Publishing, 1984), p. 35.
45. Harvey Potthoff, *God and the Celebration of Life*, p 239.
46. Daniel Simundson, *Faith Under Fire: Biblical Interpretations of Suffering* (Minneapolis: Augsurg Publishing Company, 1980), pp. 151–153.
47. Alexander Feinsilver, *Aspects of Jewish Belief* (New York: KTAV Publishing House, Inc., 1973), pp. 48, 51, 53, 54.

APPENDIX
(POLIO MEDICAL RECORDS)

CHART

THE CLINIC-HOSPITAL OF SAN ANGELO
SAN ANGELO, TEXAS

Bulbar   J+a

Hospital No. 44729
Clinic No. 14715

NAME Janek, Robert William (William W.) Sex M Room No. 202

Address Rt. 2 — Street or Route — Admitted 8-9-52 Date 10:00 Hour A.M.

San Angelo — City — Texas — State — Discharged 9-7-52 Date 10:00 Hour P.M.

Rural Telephone 1307 Birth Date July 16, 1941 Age 11 Place of Birth Texas

Marital Status M W White
*S D Colored White Religion Pro.

Date Last Adm. to Hosp. Feb. 14, 1952 Name Then

Father's Occupation Farmer Employer's Name and Address Self employed

Name of Nearest Relative Mr. Will W. Janek Address Same as above Phone Same

Who is Responsible for Bill The above mentioned Relationship Father

Address Same as above. Telephone

Adm. by Dr. Finks Referred to Doctor How Admitted

Information given by Patient's mother Registration taken by P. V. Hale

Insurance Yes

CONSENT TO TREATMENT, OPERATION AND RELEASE OF INFORMATION

This is to certify that I (We) the undersigned, hereby consent to and authorize the administration and performance of all treatments, and operations and the administration of any anesthetics which, in the judgment of my physician may be considered necessary or advisable. Further I agree that if my case is handled under the Workman's Compensation Act, Division of Interstate Commerce or any self-insured organization or mutual hospital associations, that the Insurance Carrier or Agent is hereby authorized to have access to, and to make copies of my hospital records. I further agree that the hospital authorities may give out written or verbal information to these organizations concerning my hospital records. If I should leave the hospital without the written consent of my attending physician, I hereby relieve said physician and the hospital of all responsibility for my action.

Patient's Signature

Witness By Relationship

Provisional Diagnosis 1) Left facial paralysis.
   2) ? Bells Palsey ? Polio.

Final Diagnosis 1) Polio, Acute, Bulbar.
   2) Tracheotomy.

Operation

Complications: Residual left facial paralysis.

Condition on Discharge: Recovered Improved Unimproved Observation
Died under 48 Hours Died over 48 Hours Autopsy

This is to certify that I have carefully reviewed the attached records and to the best of my knowledge find them to be accurate and correct.

11-17-52 pvh Attending Physician R. M. Finks, M. D./pvh
Consultant: C. F. Engelking, M.D.

ROBERT W. JANEK

THE CLINIC-HOSPITAL OF SAN ANGELO, SAN ANGELO, TEXAS — PERSONAL HISTORY

Name: Robert Wm Janek
Room or Ward No. 302 Bed ___ Hospital No. 44729
Date: 8-9-52 Day of Disease ___ Doctor: Finks Interne ___ Nurse ___

FINAL DIAGNOSIS: To be recorded when determined.

Age 14½ Sex M Race W S. M. W. yrs. ___ Adm ___ Dis ___
Occupation ___ Relig ___

Family History	Age	Health, if living, or cause of death. Note especially Hereditary or Infectious diseases
Father		
Mother		
Brothers		
Sisters		

Past history: Diseases from childhood to date, habits, menstrual history, social data

① Polio, Ac, Bulbar
② Tracheostomy —

Chief complaint. Date and mode of onset, probable cause, course:

Fever 24 hrs duration. Most severe headache especially over Lt. eye + some numbness of Lt. face. Fails face to Rt. when grimacing or smiling. Nausea but no vomiting. Some abdom. pain + not severe. No U.R.I. No diarrhea.

CONDITION ON DISCHARGE

Improved — Residual Lt. facial paralysis.

Former or subsequent admissions to this or other hospitals

Date	Hosp. No.	Diagnosis
1		
2		
3		

Signed: R. M. Finks
R. M. Finks, M. D./ovh

POLIO

THE CLINIC-HOSPITAL OF SAN ANGELO, SAN ANGELO, TEXAS

PHYSICAL EXAMINATION

Hosp. No. **44729**
Date **8-9-52**

Name: Robert Wm. Jamak
Room or Ward No. 202 Bed
Doctor: Fricks

Working diagnosis: After physical examination _____

General condition: Temp **100** Height ___ Wt. n ___ pr ___
Pulse: rate ___ char ___ B. P.: s ___ d ___
Resp.: rate ___ char ___
Nutrition, etc. ___

Facies and general appearance: alert, coop.
wt. while age 11 yr.

Physical findings: Head, Neck, Chest, Cardio-Vascular, Abdomen, Genito-Urinary, Skin, Bones and Joint, Glandular, Neuro-muscular.

Head — normal size & contour.
Eyes = Pupils — equal & react to L + A. EOM ok. Unable to close left eye.
Ears = normal.
Nose: mm pink — moist — no disch. or obstruction.
Oro-pharynx — mod. redness of throat, good gag reflex. Uvula draws to rt. when swallowing or talking.
Neck = moderate nuchal rigidity
Lungs = clear — resonant — todo obstruction.

Heart = sds reg & good qual — no murmurs.
Abd = neg — no tend
Genit & Ex trem = ok

Dx = Lt. facial paralysis,
? Bell's Palsy ? Polio.

Form No. 1—Holcombe-Blanton Printers
Examined by _R. M. Fricks, M. D._/pvh

ROBERT W. JANEK

History and Physical Room 103

NAME Robert Janek,   HOSPITAL NO.

DATE

C.C.: Paralysis on the left side of the face.

P.I.: Patient has had fever for the past 24 to 36 hrs. with some pain in the head, some nausea and noted some 24 hrs. ago there was a weakness on the left side of the face and this has gradually and progressively gotten worse. There has been no loss of hearing or ringing in the ears. Patient had a sore throat several days ago.

P.M.:
- Nose: Breathes through nose _none_ Operations ___ Epistaxis ___ P.N.D. _some_ Hayfever ___
  Asthma ___ Sneezing ___ Headache ___ Sense of smell ___ Injury ___
- Throat: Sore throats _one_ Tonsils in or out _Out_ Swelling of glands of neck ___ Sputum ___
  Hemoptysis ___ Hoarseness ___ Operations ___ Cough ___ Difficulty swallowing ___
  Choking ___ Condition of teeth ___
- Ears: Hearing _good_ Running ears ___ Pain ___ Operations ___ Dizziness ___
  Headache ___ Tinnitus ___ Nausea ___ Vomiting ___ Chills ___

GENERAL HEALTH: (Operations, accidents, diseases patient has had.)

SYMPTOMS: Audiometric Study reveal a ___ loss in the right ear, but perfectly normal in the left ear.
- G.I.:
- G.U.:
- Extremities:
- C.R.:
- Menses:

SOCIAL HISTORY: Drugs ___ Drinking and smoking habits ___ Veneral diseases ___

FAMILY HISTORY: History of cancer ___ Deafness in family ___ Asthma in family ___
Hayfever in family ___

E.N.T. EXAMINATION: Face: There is a definite paralysis of the side of the face, patient is showing his teeth and unable to have any wrinkles on the left cheek **
- Nose: Septum _midline_ Mucosa modit hyperemic _some_ Polyps ___ Tumor ___
  Tumor ___ Tenderness or swelling over sinuses ___
- Post. Rhin.: Pus ___ Eustachian tubes ___ Choanal ___ Pharyngeal wall ___
  Adenoids _slight amount present_
- Trans.: ** no wrinkling of the nose possible, on the forehead there is a wrinkle
- X-Ray Sinuses: on the left side, but not as marked as the right. The patient is unable to
- Puncture: close the left eye, but there is a movement there this morning. ***
- Throat: Lips ___ Teeth ___ Tongue ___ Buccal Mucosa ___
  Palate ___ Uvula ___ Tonsils _tags, bilat._ Pharynx _granular_, and moderately
- Larynx: Lingual tonsils ___ Valleculae ___ False and true cords ___ Epiglottis _hyperemic_
  Pyriform sinuses ___ Arytenoids ___ Canals _clean_ Drums _pres good light_
- Ears: Auricles ___ Post auricular region ___
  Perforations ___ Discharge ___ Swelling of posterior canal wall _reflex noted._
  Pulsations ___ Hearing ___

X-Ray Mastoids:
Heart:
Lungs: *** There is no definite loss of taste noted by the patient.
Abdomen:
Blood Pressure:
Laboratory: Wassermann:
Urinalysis:

IMPRESSIONS: POLIOMYELITIS
ATYPICAL BELL's PALSAY

RECOMMENDATIONS: OBSERVATION FOR 24 HOURS AND FURTHER STUDY FOR
DEFINITE DIAGNOSIS.

C. F. ENGELKING, M.D./su

POLIO

Record No. 44729
Name: Robert Janek
Service of Dr. R. M. Finks, M.D.

Date	N. B. Frequent Periodical Notations Should Be Made Concerning Progress of Case, Complications, Etc.
8-19-52	Patient has mild upper respiratory infection for which given injections of penicillin and streptomycin. His general condition is good. He is able to swallow a little liquid.
8-22-52	Patient has continued to have occasional nausea, is retaining food and fluids fairly well. He is able to swallow, but poorly. The facial paralysis is about the same as it has been in the past. There is slight weakness on the left deltoid. There is no other demonstrable weakness on the arms or legs.
8-25-52	Patient states that he is able to swallow fairly well. Levine tube was withdrawn. During the course of the day he took but a few bites of jell-o and a small amount of ice cream. He was unable to take fluids well; consequently the Levine tube was re-inserted.
8-28-52	Patient is now able to swallow fairly well and the Levine tube has been withdrawn.
8-30-52	Patient is eating fairly well. There is still considerable paralysis in the left face. He is as yet unable to close the left eye. There is also very slight weakness on the left shoulder.
9-3-52	Patient feels well and has continued to eat well. There is still considerable paralysis on the left face, and there is slight weakness of the left shoulder. Tracheotomy tube removed by Dr. Engelking.
9-7-52	Patient has continued to improved, seems well and feeling well. He has been up and around in his room for several days with little apparent weakness. There is still considerable left facial paralysis. There is slight weakness of the left arm. The tracheotomy wound is healing nicely.
	DISCHARGED, IMPROVED.

R. M. Finks, M.D./sn

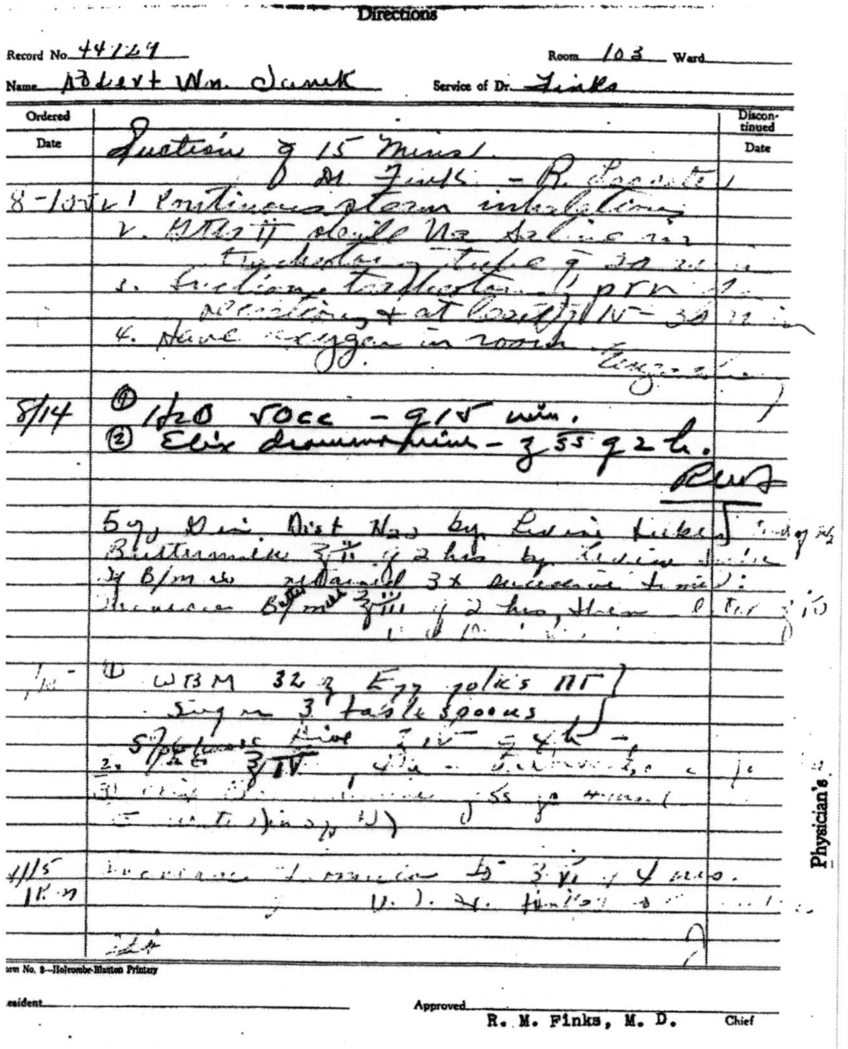

ROBERT W. JANEK

[Handwritten medical order sheet, largely illegible]

Record No. 44129　　　Room 103　Ward ___
Name: Robert Wm. Janek　　Service of Dr. Finks

Ordered Date	Directions	Discontinued Date
	Suction q 15 min.	
8-10-54	Dr. Finks — R. [illegible] 1. Continuous steam inhalation 2. [illegible] 3. Suction [illegible] q 30 [illegible], prn [illegible], & at least q IV – 30 [illegible] 4. Have oxygen in room	
8/14	① H₂O √OCC – q 15 min. ② Elix [illegible] – ℥ss q 2 h.	
	5% [illegible] Dist H₂O by [illegible] [illegible] ℥ii q 2 hrs by [illegible] [illegible] B/m [illegible] 3x [illegible] [illegible] B/m ℥iii q 2 hrs, then [illegible]	
7/[?]	① WBM 32 ℥ Egg yolks II [illegible] Sugar 3 tablespoons 2. S/p[illegible] ℥iv [illegible] 3. [illegible]	
4/15 11 A	Increase formula to ℥vi q 4 hrs. [illegible]	

Approved: R. M. Finks, M. D.　Chief

POLIO

8/11
1) Suction PRN
2) Clysis = Lactate Ringers - Alidex 500-250 cc
3) Dramamine - ℥ii gr'd rly. [illegible]

Record No. 44129   Room 132 Ward
Name Robert Wm. [illegible]   Service of Dr. Finks

Ordered Date		Discontinued Date
8/24	Dis Dramamine	
8/30	Discontinue Penicillin & strepto [illegible] Any soft foods — V.O. Dr. Finks to C.R. [illegible]	
1-3-52	Soft diet Order Dr Finks — on Burkhalter	
2-?-52	Regular Diet — ground meat & very tender [illegible] Butt V.O. Dr Finks [illegible]	
1 P.M.	[illegible] Taped in opening to trachea tube until tomorrow 4 PM. then a smaller tube to replace [illegible] V.O. Dr. Engelking	
4-5-52	Disc. hot packs 2 Hot tub bath tid. V.O. Dr. Finks P.L.	
4/7/52	Dismissed Dr Finks [illegible]	

7

BIOGRAPHICAL INFORMATION
ROBERT W. JANEK

CAREER MILESTONES
ENTWINED WITH EVER-CONTINUING INNER POLIO JOURNEY

-- 1959	Graduated Wall High School, Wall, Texas
-- 1964	Bachelor of Arts Degree in Government at Texas Technological College, Lubbock, Texas
-- 1964-1968	Commissioned an Army officer through ROTC; four years Army service, including a year in Viet Nam
-- 1968-1973	Intelligence Analyst in Defense Intelligence Agency, Washington D.C.; and did studies in International Relations at American University
-- 1975-1976	One year Clinical Internship in Pastoral Care, M.D. Anderson Cancer Center, Houston, Texas
-- 1977	Master of Divinity Degree in Specialized Ministry, Iliff School of Theology, Denver, Colorado
-- 1977	Ordained as Minister in the Unity of the Brethren denomination, Dallas, Texas
-- 1977	Ordained as Minister in the United Church of Christ denomination, Englewood, Colorado

-- 1977-1981	Team ministry with wife in St. John United Church of Christ, Idalia, Colorado
-- 1980	Master of Arts in Religion Degree in Philosophy of Religion and Theology, Iliff School of Theology, Denver, Colorado
-- 1981-1982	One year Clinical Pastoral Education Residency, Wesley Medical Center, Wichita, Kansas
-- 1982-1984	Interim Minister, Udall United Church of Christ, Udall, Kansas
-- 1982-1985	Part-time Chaplain, Veterans Administration Medical Center, Wichita, Kansas
-- 1986-1987	Part-time Hospital and Hospice Chaplain, Cushing Memorial Hospital, Leavenworth, Kansas
-- 1987-2005	Chaplain, Dwight D. Eisenhower Department of Veterans Affairs Medical Center, Leavenworth, Kansas
-- 2005	Retired and moved to his home stomping grounds in San Angelo, Texas

Robert's infectious sense of humor and genuine caring readily draw people to him, and soon they are engaging who he is, completely overlooking his facial paralysis. His presence brightens their day.

He is an avid reader, especially history, theology, philosophy, biographies, foreign affairs and the psychological aspects of the human condition.

Cats! Robert has always lived with one or two, and sometimes five or six orphan kittens.

With the San Angelo State Park bucking up to his backyard, he enjoys feeding the deer and occasional javelinas, raccoons, skunks, opossums, roadrunners, and turkeys. The deer and doves show up right on time counting on him.

His favorite quiet place on warm days at twilight is sitting on the back porch overlooking the state park and just "watching life happen." (For some reason the mosquitos never bother him!)